THE NEW VICHY
SYNDROME

THE NEW VICHY SYNDROME

Why European Intellectuals Surrender to Barbarism

THEODORE DALRYMPLE

Encounter Books New York · London

First American edition published in 2009 by Encounter Books,
an activity of Encounter for Culture and Education, Inc.,
a nonprofit, tax exempt corporation.
Encounter Books website address: www.encounterbooks.com

Manufactured in the United States and printed on
acid-free paper. The paper used in this publication meets
the minimum requirements of ANSI/NISO Z39.48–1992
(R 1997) (*Permanence of Paper*).

FIRST AMERICAN EDITION

LIBRARY OF CONGRESS CATALOGING-IN-PUBLICATION DATA
Dalrymple, Theodore.
The new Vichy syndrome : why European intellectuals surrender to barbarism /
by Theodore Dalrymple.
p. cm.
ISBN-13: 978-1-59403-372-8 (hardcover : alk. paper)
ISBN-10: 1-59403-372-2 (hardcover : alk. paper)
1. Europe, Western--Civilization—21st century. 2. Europe, Western—Intellectual life—
21st century. 3. Europe, Western—Social conditions—21st century. 4. National characteristics, European. 5. Europe, Western—Ethnic relations. 6. France—History—German
occupation, 1940-1945. I. Title.
D2021.D35 2010
940.56′1—dc22

2009041984

CONTENTS

PREFACE

The works of man from dying we may save,
But man himself moves onward to the grave.
—GEORGE CRABBE, 1823

Were we, the old connoisseurs, those who revered Europe
as it used to be, of genuine music and poetry as once they
were, nothing but a pig-headed minority suffering
from a complex neurosis, whom tomorrow would forget or
deride? Was all that we called culture, spirit, soul, all that we
called beautiful and sacred, nothing but a ghost long dead,
which only a few fools like us took for true and
living? Had it perhaps indeed never been true and living?
Had all that we poor fools bothered our heads about
never been anything but a phantom?
—HERMANN HESSE, *STEPPENWOLF*, 1927

Anyone who would be creative must have the self-confidence to plough his own furrow and the humility to accept justified criticism. This, as anyone who has tried it will confirm, is a difficult balance to achieve. Arrogance on the one hand and meek submission to the opinion of critics on the other are twin deformations to be avoided and are in dialectical relationship to one another. It is easy to swing, pendulum-like, between the two.

Likewise, a civilization must be open to outside influences if it is not to become self-satisfied in a state of inanition, but not so open that it can see nothing in its own achievements worthy of preservation. No trick is harder to pull off than to conserve while changing.

Western Europe is in a strangely neurotic condition, of being smug and anxious at the same time, or of veering suddenly between complacency and despond and back again. On the one hand, it believes that it has at last created a social and political system that, give or take a reform or two, is the full and final answer to the age-old question of how man is to live in society. Such serious social problems as persist are not the consequences of its system, but hangovers from the past that can be reformed out of existence.

On the other hand, there is anxiety that Europe is falling behind in a globalized world in which non-participation in the race is not an option, especially for an overpopulated region without sufficient natural resources even to feed itself, let alone live at the high standard of living to which it has become accustomed and the achievement of which it now sees as the main purpose of human existence.

Europe wants, as of right, both security and luxury in a world that neither can nor wants to grant it either. Understanding and denying this at the same time, it looks forward with apprehension but does nothing practical to meet the challenges. It is like the rabbit mesmerized by the stoat: it wishes the dangers would simply go away and not come back again.

But while it fears the future, it hates the past. The reasons are not difficult to discern. There is disappointment that the continent is no longer the center of the world, as it was for some hundreds of years, a position to which it long thought it was entitled; but, in addition, the history of the past century (the twentieth) seems nothing but a catalogue of catastrophe. Let me here quote the classicist Goldsworthy Lowes Dickinson, in his introduction to his popular lectures *Plato and His Dialogues*, published in 1931:

> I have never met a young man who passed through [the Great War], or grew up after it, who has any belief in progress at all.

The very concept of progress, applied either to the future or to the past, is illusory or naïve; and therefore the past is but a prelude to or preparation for the events that exposed the illusion for what it was. And this was before the Second World War, which was the icing on the cake of despair, as it were.

The habit of seeing in the past no *gloire*, but only whatever leads up to our present discontents, has become general and widespread with the extension of education and the diffusion of information through the media of mass communication. A kind of miserabilist historiography has become the mark of the sensitive and well-informed, proof against any facile optimism about the past. I came across a fine example, almost a *reductio ad absurdum*, of this way of looking at things in Paris recently, where I picked up a book by the writer Patrick Besson, called *Haine de la Hollande*.

Besson is a Serbophile, who sees both NATO's war against Serbia and the subsequent trial of Slobodan Milosevic as wrong. As it happens, I agree with him; the war, begun on a lying pretext, by an arrogant ultimatum designed to be unacceptable to its recipient, solved no problem, and was won only by the resort to the very crimes of which Serbia was accused, i.e. the bombing of civilian targets. It also brought about the very ethnic cleansing that it was supposedly designed to stop. As for the trial of Milosevic, it invented a new kind of kangaroo court, one whose summary and pre-ordained verdict took years to arrive at, at an immense financial cost—a court that made up its procedural rules to suit the verdict as it went along.

M. Besson allows himself to hate Holland, however, because the trial took place in the Hague. His book starts with the following words:

> First, the geographical point of view. On the map, it is a ridiculous little piece of cheese gnawed by mice.

It does not even cross M. Besson's mind that the creation of a country that has been one of the richest and freest in the world for hundreds of years might actually constitute a triumph of the human spirit.

Then there is the history:

> The Dutch began their career in the history of the world by collaboration with the Romans. They resisted the Franks no better who, indicating by their prescience the intrinsic value of this superior race, quickly judged the Dutch climate disgusting and removed to the south, as far as the Seine, where they felt better.

I wish that I could say that this was all meant ironically, but the book was printed in Serbia; and whatever else one might say about the Serbs, their xenophobia is rarely a matter of irony. Besides, the book continues:

> Some distinguished liars have tried to make us believe that there was, from 1600 to 1700, a Dutch "Golden Age." It is a grotesque fable. Let us take, for example, Vermeer, the petit bourgeois painter par excellence, capable of spending six months painting a servant pouring some milk. Vermeer is heavy, narrow, empty and even stupid. His poetry has no heart, his intelligence no balls. He is as cold as a condemned man. It is technique put at the service of the void, a sort of of cinematic Hollywood production before its time.

As for Rembrandt, he is no better: "morbidly emphatic," "nauseatingly grandiloquent."

During "the so-called Golden Age," the Dutch "took advantage of the lack of liberty elsewhere in Europe to enrich themselves by publishing, in editions of a quality less than mediocre, works forbidden elsewhere" (such as Descartes and Laclos, for example).

Here is how a man who describes Belgrade as "sacred" describes Amsterdam, whose domestic architecture is surely some of the greatest ever produced by mankind:

> Amsterdam is a humid death-chamber where the only people who show a bit of life or warmth are the countless African, Asian and Arab prostitutes, drowned in beer or soft drugs. Amsterdam is a nostalgia with neither subject nor object. It lies between softness and death. Adipose civil servants, gouty retirees and stupid tourists wander along its canals in silence which, by their very mediocrity, discourage suicide. Amsterdam smells of French fries, its women, of course, of mussels.

This is all as if someone who disagreed with American foreign policy said that, therefore, Tennessee Williams couldn't write plays, Audubon couldn't paint birds, and Edison was uninventive.

In fact this kind of historiography, which traces a current discontent or complaint backwards and then claims it to be the whole of history, is now predominant. The number of grievance-bearers is so great that it includes almost the whole of the population, and is much increased since mass immigration so greatly balkanized the populations Europe. In Europe, even the rich and powerful can now imagine themselves to be an oppressed minority.

A belief that one's history contains nothing good or worthwhile leads either to utopian dreams of a new beginning, or a failure to resist those utopian dreams: in other words to fanaticism or apathy. Fanaticism is resentment in search of power; consumerism is apathy in search of happiness.

Out of Africa, always something new; out of Europe, what exactly? Collapse? Extremism?

I.

SOMETHING ROTTEN

There is something is rotten in the state of Europe, but it is not easy to say what it is or where it comes from. Partly it is difficult because, short of the Big Bang, the Garden of Eden, or the Unmoved Mover, there is no final cause of anything; when tracing back the origin of social or political problems, it is always open to someone to say that the origin had its own origin in turn, and that *this* is therefore the *real*, the *true*, origin.

It is strange that Europe should be the sick man of Europe. In many ways, things have never been better on the old continent; to take but one illustration of this fact, life expectancy has never been higher. When my father was born, in 1909, his life expectancy was forty-nine; if he had been born today, his life expectancy would be approaching eighty. No doubt Keats, Schubert, and Mozart packed a lot into their lives, but most people would nonetheless opt for long rather than short life spans.

The increase in wealth and the physical standard of living has been startling, moreover; in 1960, Sicilian peasants still slept indoors with their farm animals, and my working-class patients remembered sharing outside lavatories with several other households. In France, the years in which it lost its colonial empire are known as *les trente glorieuses*, the glorious thirty, when the French economy grew so fast that absolute poverty was eliminated and the country obtained one of the best infrastructures in the world. Germany's *Wirtschaftswunder* after the war really was a wonder; it was spoken of without cynicism, and transformed a country that the US Secretary of the Treasury, Henry Morgenthau, Jr., wanted to keep forever in a state of rural pre-industrialization into the largest exporter of manufactured goods in the world, a remarkable achievement. It did this, moreover, while creating the very model of a model liberal-democratic state.

And yet, for all this success, there is a pervasive sense of impending doom, or at least of decline, in Europe. For example, as a European, I cannot help but feel how far and how fast the continent is falling behind the rest of the world whenever I visit Singapore, Peking, or even Dubai.[1]

---

1. The latter is built, of course, with an almost limitless supply of Indian migrant labor. Even for someone such as I who is by no means an egalitarian, the disparity between the enormous wealth of a few privileged people, natives of the place who were fortunate to be born in such a place at such a time, and the stringent conditions under which the Indian workers live, induces unease. I once bought a Tanzanite ring at a jeweler's there for my wife, and while the price I offered for it was being relayed to the owner of the shop for his approval or otherwise, I talked to the Indian shop assistant who was dealing with me about his life. He worked fourteen hours a day, six days a week; his wages were low, and I discovered that I (sometimes) earned more as a free-lance journalist in an hour than he in a year. His accommodation was rudimentary, and he had only a week's (unpaid) holiday a year. I imagine that, as a salesman of jewelery with knowledge of his trade, his pay was by no means the lowest, nor his conditions of work the most onerous, to be found in Dubai at the time.

Yet he did not give the impression of unhappiness, let alone misery. To me, whom he might easily have considered a spoilt and pernickety brat, he was charming and courteous. And when I murmured some kind of sympathy for him, he brushed it aside, saying that he had come to Dubai voluntarily, that he had decided that, all things considered, it was better than staying at home in his native Bombay, and that his wages—low as they were—allowed him to save something for his marriage, opening up the possibility of starting a business in a few years' time when he returned.

This, of course, is precisely the answer that critics of Dubai would give (I do not here deal with criticism of the vacuity of the shopping and vulgar luxury that draw people to the place). The Arabs of the Emirates do not employ slave, but free, labor, and for all the stories of abuse and exploitation, it keeps coming. No doubt it would be possible for individual employers to raise their wages and still get everything done at a profit. But that does not

I am not concerned here to endorse the social or political arrangements of these places, or assert that I wish to copy them, let alone live in them. I remark merely on the strength of their economies, on the obvious energy and intelligence that they are able to engage at all levels of the population. Compare how a laborer works in England with how his equivalent works in China or Singapore! The latter works urgently, putting his heart and soul into his work, as if something important depended upon it. He is participating in something larger than himself. For the former, there is nothing larger, or at any rate more important, than himself, and therefore he is in no hurry and feels little compulsion, either internal or external, to exert himself mightily. Whatever the explanation for the extreme, urgent, and nervous energy displayed by workers in the East, I do not think that external compulsion can be the whole, or even the major part, of it. Slave labor, after all, is not particularly efficient. Nor am I saying that this energy is wholly good, beneficial, or attractive in itself. There is clearly more to the good life than working fantastically, one might even say fanatically, hard,[2] though we should not underestimate, either, the importance of work as a source of self-respect.

No, when a European sees all this energy he knows that his continent cannot hope to match it, as surely as an aging man knows when he sees a young athlete in his prime that he cannot

---

alter the fundamental argument. Nor do these considerations affect my basic point: I am not remarking on the justice of the social arrangements of Dubai, but upon its manifest vigor although the current crisis has exposed the fragility of its model of development.

2. One of the first poems I had to commit to memory as a child—it was not yet absolutely believed that rote learning was a form of child abuse—was one by W. H. Davies:

What is this life if, full of care,
We have no time to stand and stare? —

No time to stand beneath the boughs,
And stare as long as sheep and cows . . .

A poor life this if, full of care,
We have no time to stand and stare.

No doubt a banal sentiment, but surely one not without some truth. Strange how potent cheap poetry is.

hope ever to rival his loose-limbed strength or grace. His best days are behind him, and it is little consolation to him that he is now, thanks to his age, wiser, richer, or less tormented by ambition than the younger man.

Should this matter? No one travelling through Europe would conclude from what he saw that life there was unbearable, far from it. In many countries, on the contrary, life seems distinctly good. The people are healthy (the Dutch are by now the tallest people in the world, a tribute to the abundance, if not to the excellence, of food there), they do not have to work excessively to survive, they are housed and warmed, they have disposable income enough to secure their entertainments, of which there is a greater choice than ever before. Viewed from the perspective of absolute standards, there is nothing much to be morose about.

Alas—or perhaps it is a good thing—man is a comparing animal, at least when he has the knowledge necessary to compare himself with others: which, in these times of unprecedented access to information (indeed, it is not necessary nowadays to go to information; it will come to you whether you want it or not), and of mass travel, he is more than ever liable to make comparisons. What makes him happy is not so much a high standard of living for himself, as a higher standard of living than someone else. As Gore Vidal remarked, it is not sufficient that I should succeed, it is necessary that someone else should fail. And this applies not only to the standard of living, but to achievements of other kinds.

The awareness that the gap between Europe and much of the rest of the world, in point of both wealth and achievement in other spheres, has dramatically decreased, and in some instances reversed, was bound to give rise to unease, even if it was regarded as inevitable in the long run.[3] No one likes to see his place in the pecking order decline.

But there are even darker worries haunting Europe. It is one thing to fret over a decline that leads you to inhabit a static,

---

3. "The Continent of Europe," said Disraeli in 1838, "will not suffer England to be the workshop of the world." What was true of England and the Continent soon became true of the Continent and the rest of the world.

but rich and genteel, country that is more like museum of past achievement than a living, breathing power,[4] but another to contemplate absolute decline. For once the machinery of international competition is set up, there is no standing still: you can go only forwards or backwards. If you don't keep up, you will go back, not relatively but absolutely, and Europe is blessed neither with natural resources nor huge tracts of virgin land upon which its population might lead a simpler life than that demanded by advanced economies.

ANXIETY

The arrival of at least two giant industrial nations on the scene—India and China—disquiets Europeans for three reasons. The first is that it is inherently difficult to compete with the combination of cheap labor and high technology; the second is that the only means of doing so, by technological advance that keeps ahead of the competition, looks increasingly beyond the continent's capacity. The continent that invented science as a self-conscious method of accumulating more knowledge about nature and the means by which it might be used to achieve human ends (evil as well as good, of course) has increasingly lost its position of leadership, and is now reduced to the application of what others discover or develop. A crude illustration of the decline of European science is the ratio of the number of Nobel Prizes won by British and American scientists in the fields of physics and chemistry for the periods 1940–1975 and 1976–2005. (British scientists were the most prolific winners of Nobel Prizes in Europe.) In the former period, British scientists won 37.5 percent as many prizes for physics as American scientists; in the latter period, 4.5 percent. For chemistry the figures were 93.3 percent and 16.7 percent respectively. Moreover, the figures declined not only relatively, but

---

4. This discomfiting thought is expressed very forcibly in, for example, *La France qui tombe*, Nicolas Baverez, Perrin, 2003.

absolutely: from 9 to 2 in the case of physics, and from 14 to 6 in the case of chemistry.[5]

No doubt the relation between success in pure science and industrial or economic prowess is not a straightforward one. Entire countries have overtaken Britain economically without contributing a twentieth as much as Britain to the sum total of man's scientific knowledge. Not only Britain, however, but the whole of Europe cannot be said to be in the forefront of world technology, either, though there may be isolated areas in which it leads. And this relative decline—which in some cases may even be absolute—is both humiliating in itself and bodes ill in a competitive world. Moreover, there is not much confidence anywhere that change for the better is at hand, or indeed that anyone knows, even in principle, let along practice, how to bring it about. I shall explore the deep-seated reasons for this later in the book.

The third cause for anxiety in Europe over the rise of India, China, and other lesser, but still considerable, countries as competitors is Europe's strategic vulnerability. It is almost entirely dependent for its energy on foreign and distant resources. These resources are in areas or countries that are either politically unstable or potentially hostile—competition for their resources could easily turn acute. The economic downturn that caused a decline in the price of oil will probably not last forever, as downturns in the past have not lasted for ever;[6] and often a period of

---

5. On a brighter note, awards of the Nobel Peace Prize to British citizens or organizations have increased by 250 percent, admittedly from a low base. Not everyone will rejoice at this, since the prize seems often to be awarded to those who refrain from indulging in or encouraging the violence that they previously indulged in or encouraged.

6. What has happened in the past is not an infallible guide to the future, of course, but is probably better than no guide at all. In the heady days of the last economic boom, I read several newspaper commentators, more knowledgeable in economics than I (not difficult), who thought that the business cycle had finally been overcome by the virtuous circle of higher productivity on the one hand and constantly increasing demand on the other, while the central banks and regulatory authorities had now become sufficiently sophisticated and armed with past experience to prevent serious recessions, let alone 1929-type catastrophes. Having read Charles Mackay's *Memoirs of Extraordinary Popular Delusions and the Madness of Crowds*, I did not believe it; but my reasons for not believing it were insufficient. Nevertheless, I was right to be skeptical.

exuberant growth follows. Then competition for energy resources will be fierce, and resort to force or the threat of force might be necessary. How would Europe fare if such an eventuality came to pass?

Europe is not only non-militaristic, it is anti-military.[7] The profession of arms has no prestige whatever; on the contrary, it has the very reverse of prestige. No thought is more alien to the modern European mind, brought up in a lasting peace that followed two of the most catastrophic wars in history, than that he who desires peace must prepare for war. Even to entertain such a thought is to be branded a warmonger, as someone who secretly or openly glorifies the cull of young men, and increasingly of others, known as war.

WEAKNESS

A lack of military preparedness and capablity, however, has its consequences. When, in the wake of the Danish cartoon affair, the Danish embassy in Damascus was attacked with the obvious connivance of the Syrian government, how did, how could, Europe respond? The impression was given, and it was a correct one, that Europe had no means of dealing with a couple of cunning and treacherous mullahs who stirred up trouble for Denmark, other than by virtually giving in to demands that certain important subjects henceforth be placed, *de facto,* off limits for discussion. Even if the policy of appeasement were not officially enunciated, what was made abundantly clear by the whole episode was that there would be no retaliation by European countries for threats made to their own citizens: and that there would be no retaliation because there could be no retaliation. The quiet life was clearly preferred to the costs of securing a free one; if only we appeased enough, there would be peace in our time.

---

7. I assume here that there is a difference between militarism, that is to say seeing the army as the guiding institution of a country or state, and a condition of military preparedness.

Europe has hardly navy enough to suppress the Somali pirates, let alone protect its interests against a more serious ill-wisher with a hold over its energy supplies. Merely because bellicosity is a vice, cowardice is not a virtue. Nor will the latter earn the respect, but rather the contempt, of those who do not share an anti-military point of view.

Prosperous as never before, long-lived as never before, Europeans look into the future with anxiety or even with fear, as if they had a secret sickness that had not yet made itself manifest by obvious symptoms or signs but that was nevertheless eating them away in their vital parts. They are aware that, in Chinese parlance, the mandate of heaven has been withdrawn from them; and in losing that, they have lost everything. All that is left to them is to preserve their remaining privileges as best they can; *après nous*, as a well-known mistress of Louis XV is said to have remarked, *le deluge.*

2.

DEMOGRAPHIC WORRIES, OR THE DEARTH OF BIRTH AND ITS CONSEQUENCES

In *The Sonnets*, Shakespeare tells the young man to whom they are addressed that he must have children, in particular a son, or else he has lived in vain, indeed badly and selfishly. The very first lines of the sequence are:

> From fairest creatures we desire increase,
> That thereby beauty's rose might never die . . .

The message is conveyed *ad* what would be *nauseam* were it not for Shakespeare's sublime poetic gift:

> Be not self-willed, for thou art much too fair
> To be death's conquest and make worms thine heir.

Or:

> Is it for fear to wet a widow's eye
> That thou consum'st thyself in single life?
> Ah, if thou issueless shalt hap to die,
> The world will wail thee like a makeless wife,
> The world will be thy widow and still weep.

Or:

> Who lets so fair a house fall to decay,
> Which husbandry in honour might uphold
> Against the stormy gusts of winter's day
> And barren rage of death's eternal cold?
> O none but unthrifts! Dear my love you know,
> You had a father; let your son say so.

In fact, I could cite scores of passages that convey this, or a closely allied thought, which for most of human history has been a commonplace: namely, that the passing on of one's life to another generation is both part of what makes human life worth living, and testimony that it is in fact worth living.

But modern Europeans, it seems, do not agree. They are not concerned to replace themselves, and have other things on their minds. Here are the fertility rates of several European countries in 2004:

Ireland: 1.99
France: 1.90
Norway: 1.81
Sweden 1.75
UK: 1.74
Netherlands: 1.73
Germany: 1.37
Italy: 1.33
Spain: 1.32
Greece: 1.29

The replacement fertility rate for developed countries such as those in the above list is generally taken to be 2.1.[8] Not a single western European country, therefore, has a fertility rate that will ensure that its population will maintain itself at its current size.

Moreover, life expectancy is continuing to rise. Some of the countries with the lowest fertility rates (Spain and Italy, for example) have among the highest life expectancies in the world, and they are still rising. This rise in turn raises fears that the economically active proportion of the population will decline, and that those unfortunate enough still to be in employment will have to devote ever more of their labor-time to the maintenance of the numerous aging drones in their midst. This will create tensions, all the more so as the youth culture which, paradoxically, predominates in an aging population is not exactly solicitous or respectful of the comfort, opinions, and welfare of the elderly.

IMMIGRANTS INSTEAD OF CHILDREN

One solution, joyously embraced by some, especially by liberal intellectuals, but feared by the majority, is mass immigration from far-away countries of which we know nothing. Europe has always known population movements, of course, peaceful, violent, horrific, beneficial, as the case may be.[9] But yet the type of mass immigration that it has experienced recently is of a different type, that renders large cities unfamiliar to those who grew up in them. This is anxiety-provoking in itself; we have enough change to assimilate in the technological sphere without the added anxieties produced by not understanding the basic cultural, ethical, and social assumptions of our neighbors.

---

8. It is marginally higher than 2 because, of course, some children die before they can reproduce. The more children who die before the age of reproduction, the higher the replacement fertility rate.

9. My mother and my paternal grandparents were refugees to Britain. My wife's paternal grandparents were refugees to France. In any middle-class social gathering in Britain or France, especially in intellectual circles or those of the liberal professions, it is astonishing how much population movement there is in the ancestry of the participants.

In particular, of course, there are deep and often unspoken anxieties about the size and increase in the Moslem population of Europe. This population is younger than the native, or non-Moslem, population;[10] it is constantly being enlarged by what are known as "fetching" marriages, that is to say marriages in which a resident Moslem finds a bride or a groom in his ancestral land and then, under family reunification rules, brings her or him to Europe; and finally, the fertility rate among Moslems is feared to be much higher than the native population.

Therefore, when the French newspapers reported, in a triumphant and even triumphalist way that the birth rate in France had recently become the highest in Europe (though still not quite reaching the replacement rate), publishing cartoons to accompany the reports of a rejuvenated Marianne[11] baring her arm and flexing her demographic biceps, there was a ghost at the banquet: that is to say, the proportion of babies born to Moslem mothers. There was not a single word on this delicate subject; it would have been an intellectual and moral solecism to mention it. Instead, the articles suggested that the figures represented a triumph for the French welfare state, which allegedly made it easier, more comfortable, or more economically advantageous for women to have children than anywhere else in Europe.

The same ghost was notable by its absence from the paper by the French National Institute for Statistical and Economic Studies, entitled *Demographic balance sheet: a record natural increase*. The Institute faced both practical and ethical problems, the practical problem being that French census and registration data do not contain information about the religious affiliations of French citizens. The ethical problem was that of the danger of throwing fuel on a fire, or even of starting the fire itself, if such information

---

10. Terminology is difficult here, and getting more difficult. Moslems of the second generation are, of course, native, in the sense of having been born in the territory and of having no other citizenship than that of the land of their birth.

11. The Britannia of France. She always looks slightly cross to me, as do most mythological embodiments of whole countries, as if their populations did not quite live up to their ideals—which, of course, they do not. At any rate, I don't think Marianne, or Britannia for that matter, would be much fun at a dinner party.

had been gathered and made available, for example by surveying the given names of those born in the country over a determined period, which would surely have given a rough idea of the proportion of children born to Moslem parents.

SOMETHING MISSING

But it is certainly not difficult to find anxieties expressed by the French and others about the demographic evolution of France. Wild speculations and statements abound and flourish in an atmosphere in which hard data are sometimes difficult to come by, because the French state insists that once someone becomes French by citizenship, his ancestors become, metaphorically speaking, the Gauls, and he is therefore not to be distinguished from any other Frenchman, in statistics or anywhere else. It would take considerable conceptional subtlety as well as empirical knowledge to disentangle the truth and lies of all this.

Let us now turn to the question of how far demographic fears are justified. Here it is essential to make a general point: a projection is not a prediction. What has happened in the past may not happen in the future; what has not happened in the past may happen in the future. Nothing is easier than to provoke anxiety and alarm than by extending ever upwards the line of a graph showing exponential growth, until some impossible and catastrophic situation is reached.

If you seed a Petri dish containing the right growth medium with the bacterium *Staphylococcus aureus*, the colony will grow at such a rate that, if it were to continue, the whole of the biosphere would soon consist of nothing else but *Staphylococcus aureus*. But—of course—that does not happen. The germ does not take over the world because the conditions necessary for its exponential growth do not continue to hold. If you look at the history of recent failed apocalyptic predictions (and there is nothing modern man seems to like more, to judge from the sale of books, than the contemplation of his own species-annihilation), they fail because the authors have not appreciated sufficiently the difference between a projection and a prediction. Within my lifetime, the earth has been destined to freeze over or heat up to the point that the planet will be uninhabitable for humans,[12] population has been destined to rise so fast that mass famine on an unprecedented scale was literally inevitable, the spread of AIDS was to decimate the population of the world without anybody being able to do anything about it, and hundreds of thousands if not millions of my countrymen were doomed to contract a variant of Creutzfeld-Jakob disease because of having eaten meat infected with mad cow disease. No doubt there were many other predicted apocalypses of which I failed to take notice, and everyone will have his favorite. While it is no doubt true that there might one day be such an apocalypse, if only a fraction of what was predicted in the last three decades to happen had actually happened it would have gone hard for the human race. Instead, it has flourished—to the point at which its flourishing is itself the precondition of further inevitable apocalypses.

Bearing this in mind, let us consider the premises of the demographic gloom that has overtaken Europe and (more especially) commentators about Europe.

APOCALYPSE SOON, OR NOT

First, there is the unexamined assumption that a successful country—successful in the economic sense—must have a large and expanding population.

Certainly, large populations are not necessary for economic success. Singapore and Hong Kong are among the most successful

---

12. Cf. Robert Frost:

Some say the world will end in fire,
Some say in ice.
From what I've tasted of desire
I hold with those who favor fire.
But if it had to perish twice,
I think I know enough of hate
To say that for destruction ice
Is also great
And would suffice.

economies in the world, which in the relatively short space of forty years far outstripped in productivity the economy of the colonizing nation, Britain. Denmark, a country with neither a large nor fast-expanding population, has an economy more successful than that of the United States.

For many years, countries with large and fast-expanding populations experienced little economic growth. Nigeria has the largest population in Africa by far, but its economy is spectacularly unsuccessful despite[13] huge oil revenues.

In other words, a large and expanding population is neither a necessary nor a sufficient cause of economic success, and may in fact have nothing whatever to do with economic success. Access to large markets may be another matter: but a large population does not necessarily in itself constitute a large market.

Second, while there is obviously some connection between a large, youthful population and military power, the relationship is not by any means a straightforward one. Technology and morale are as important as manpower, and no numbers will supply the want of the former. Britain defeated China in the Opium War,[14] despite having a population no more than 5 percent of the Celestial Empire's.

Third, the view of an aging population as necessarily one in which there are increasing numbers of economic drones might not be accurate either. Contrary to the miserabilist contention that a longer life is inevitably one with a longer period of pain, suffering, and incapacity, the tendency has been not only for people to live longer, but to enjoy better health as they do so. The longer they live, in fact, the more years of good health that they enjoy. Governments have therefore felt not only the necessity, but the tolerability, of delaying the age of retirement because of increased life expectancies. People are now able to work well beyond the

---

13. Here I think a good case could be made out for the replacement of "despite" by "because of."

14. A defeat that must surely be applauded by all those who believe in man's inalienable right to intoxicate himself with anything he pleases. In this respect, the war certainly led to an increase in freedom for the average Chinese.

age at which they would once have been considered old.[15] This is bad news if you hate your work and regard it merely as an unfortunate means to an end, but it is good news if your work is an important source of satisfaction to you. It has long been known that doctors who retire at the last possible moment, at the age beyond which their institutions will no longer employ them, can expect a very short retirement, dying soon afterwards. Continued work, presumably, would have prolonged their lives; at any rate, the evidence suggests that an active life, socially, culturally, and intellectually, is conducive to general health. While it is true that strenuous manual labor is likely to remain beyond the capacities of the elderly, such labor is not exactly the wave of the future for advanced economies. It is not necessarily true, therefore, that an aging population must contain an ever-increasing ratio of inactive to active members of the population, let alone that the inactive should represent an impossible millstone for the active. Furthermore, if my own case is anything to go by, one's desire to consume declines with age: one grows satisfied and possession does not seem nine-tenths of happiness any more.

It is as well to remember also—a very different point—that the aging of the population might not continue. Just because life expectancy has increased more or less continually over the past century does not necessarily mean that it will continue to do so. Bertrand Russell makes this point when he discusses the problem of (logical) induction in his brief introductory book, first published in 1912, *The Problems of Philosophy*.

> We know that all these rather crude expectations of uniformity are liable to be misleading. The man who has fed the chicken every day throughout its life at last wrings its neck instead, showing that more refined views as to the uniformity of nature would have been useful to the chicken.

---

15. When I qualified as a doctor in 1974, geriatricians took patients over the age of 65. By the time of my (early) retirement, they took patients only after the age of 80, and by no means all of them at that.

In other words, a continued increase in life expectancy, while possible and perhaps even probable, is not intrinsically irreversible. Nature is perfectly capable of developing little surprises for us that upset our calculations: the best laid schemes of mice and men oft go awry. It is as well to remember the last stanza of the poem from which this old saw is adapted, Robert Burns' "To a Mouse, On Turning Her up in Her Nest with the Plough":

Still thou art blest, compar'd wi' me
The present only toucheth thee:
But, Och! I backward cast my e'e.
On prospects drear!
An' forward, tho' I canna see,
I guess an' fear!

In guessing, and fearing, we are inclined to forget man's enormous adaptability. I have often forgotten it myself. About a quarter of a century ago, after a brief visit to Egypt, I wrote an article for a well-known British publication pointing out that 1 percent of Egypt's remaining arable land was being used every year for building, and that the population was increasing by 3 percent a year. In my best Cassandra style, I predicted disaster: famine and mass starvation for a country whose habitable portion was the size of Wales, yet whose population was destined soon to be larger than that of Great Britain and the Netherlands combined.

When was the famine, where is the starvation? Ah, give it another quarter century, you say, and it will come (though the rate of increase in the population has halved). We forget that there is a ghoulish pleasure in contemplating apocalyptic epidemics, famines, and wars. We are like latterday Augustines, who pray, "Lord, bring the end, but not just yet!"

3.

THEY BREED LIKE . . .

Let us now turn to the Moslem demographics of Europe and the fears that they often arouse—or hopes, for that matter, among those who want to see the green flag of Islam fly everywhere, in the fatuous hope or expectation that all human problems will be resolved thereby, a hope or expectation that, even if not refuted by the most elementary reflection on human nature, is belied by the history of Islam from its very first years.[16]

The wildest fear is as follows: that the Moslem population of Europe is younger and much more fecund than the rest of the population, and that therefore, before very long, Europe will become Islamized or Islamic by sheer weight of numbers. It is not

---

16. Three of the four so-called "Rightly-guided Caliphs," those who were the direct successors of Mohammed, were assassinated, two by rebel groups. Mohammed's favorite wife, Aisha, is said to have encouraged the rebels against Uthman, by whom he was assassinated. What would we say of a modern polity three of whose four heads of government were assassinated in a matter of twenty-nine years, two of them by those who had taken up arms against them? I do not think perfection is the word that would come to mind, nor would it be deemed a model to be emulated.

difficult to find alarmist statements to the effect that the process is already so far advanced as to be unstoppable, which is hardly surprising when luminaries such as the Archbishop of Canterbury, the head of a church that calls itself apostolic and universal, allows himself to say over the BBC that adoption of Sharia law in Britain now seems unavoidable,[17] and indeed desirable.

The fertility rate of women born in the Netherlands and still residing in the Netherlands was 1.6 in 1990 and 1.7 in 2005. The figures for women born in Morocco but residing in the Netherlands for those years were, respectively, 4.9 and 2.9. Downward trends in fertility are seen in all Islamic countries, and are likely at some stage to reach or go below replacement level. (Of course, this is a projection, not a forecast known to be true.) Thus, in countries such as the Netherlands which have made it more difficult for immigrants to enter, and assuming what cannot be certain, namely that current trends continue smoothly, the proportion of the population that is Moslem is likely to rise for a time, and then stabilize. Austria presents a similar picture.

In France, which has the largest Moslem population in Europe by far, the total picture is difficult to grasp. About half its five million (or so) Moslems are not citizens. Between 1991 and 1998, the fertility rate for all women residing in France was 1.7, while that of foreign-born women was 1.86. For women born in Turkey it was 3.21, in Algeria 2.57, in Morocco 2.97, and in Tunisia 2.9.

---

17. It is not always easy to know quite what the Archbishop means, and I suspect that he has the same problem himself. Murkiness, alas, is not the same as profundity, in prose as in water. To illustrate, I quote a typical passage from his lecture to eminent lawyers in London entitled *Civil and Religious Law in England—a Religious Perspective*: "The rule of law is thus not the enshrining of priority for the universal/abstract dimension of social existence but the establishing of a space accessible to everyone in which it is possible to affirm and defend a commitment to human dignity *as such*, independent of membership in any specific human community or tradition, so that when specific communities or traditions are in danger of claiming finality for their own boundaries of practice and understanding, they are reminded that they have to come to terms with the actuality of human diversity— and that the only way of doing this is to acknowledge the category of 'human dignity as such'—a non-negotiable assumption that each agent (with his or her historical and social affiliations) could be expected to have a voice in the shaping of some common project for the well-being and order of a human group." With the Archbishop, we not only see, but read through a glass darkly.

Women born in Turkey but living in France had more children than Turkish women staying in Turkey; this was also true of Tunisians, but the reverse was true of Algerians and Moroccans, who had fewer children if they lived in France. The interpretation or meaning of the fact that Turkish and Tunisian women have more children in France than in their native countries is not straightforward or self-evident: they might come from sub-populations of whom this is not true (as, of course, might the women from Algeria and Morocco who have fewer children in France than in their native lands).

DEMOGRAPHIC COUNTER-REVOLUTION

Still, declining fertility seems for the moment to be the pattern; the total fertility rate in several Moslem countries is now below that of France before the 1960s. The demographic transition, as it is known, is the result of forces far more powerful than that of the desire of some Moslems for Islamic domination of the world. Assuming, therefore, that Europe as a whole finds the way, and the will, to limit fresh immigration from Moslem countries, there is reason to believe that the proportion of Moslems in the population will stabilize, at a higher proportion than now no doubt, but still at minority levels.[18] Demographic change is not the threat to the survival of Europe that it is sometimes claimed to be.

IMMIGRANTS CHANGE

There is another consideration that should give pause to those who see Islamization, at any rate other than that brought about by numbers alone, as the most fundamental threat to the continu-

---

18. The limitation may also be brought about spontaneously, by the hidden hand of the market. Lack of economic opportunity might also make Europe less attractive as a destination of the desperate, though it must be admitted that conditions in Europe would have to deteriorate pretty far, and conditions in Africa improve pretty fast, for it to cease being the cynosure of many an African's eye.

ation of Europe as a civilization: the assumption that the experience of migration to, and subsequent life in, Europe does nothing to change the Moslems themselves, and that, in fact, their religious affiliation is of such overwhelming importance to them that nothing else goes into forming and maintaining their identity. This, I think, is far too crude and pessimistic a view. Indeed, it seems to me likely that Islamism in Europe is a reaction to cultural dislocation caused by the very power of the dislocating attractions (many of which seem to me to be in truth, *sub specie aeternitatis,* not very attractive) that Moslem youth experience merely by living in Europe. I shall return to Islamism in a moment.

But first the question of whether religion is always and everywhere the organizing principle of Moslems' sense of identity: that is to say, once you are a Moslem, nothing else counts for you, at least not much. The answer to this question is no.

The largest group of Moslems living in the Netherlands is of Indonesian origin, but of them little is heard because they are law-abiding and religiously undemanding. The Islam of Indonesia is famously—or notoriously, depending on your point of view—mild and unfanatical, or was until recently. The possibility that it might change in the direction of rigor, a change that some claim is already happening, does not alter the logical point, that Islam does not always consume those who profess it to the exclusion of all else.

Surveys in France have found that more than a half of French Moslems feel that their primary identity is French rather than Islamic. Most have a good or favorable impression of the country. Perhaps this is not surprising, since attendance at the mosque among them is high only by the standards of church attendance in one of the most irreligious countries in Europe. A fifth of Moslems in France marry out of the religion, and while it is possible that some of them require the conversion of their spouses as a condition of marriage, it is also likely that many of them are expressing an indifference to their religion by their choice of marriage partner.

Of course, the meaning of survey evidence is not always clear. People may lie about their real feelings or beliefs, despite all promises of anonymity. The relation between their answers, even if indicative of their true beliefs and feelings, and their conduct is unknown. After all, we most of us have beliefs and feelings, even strong ones, upon which we do not act, indeed beliefs and feelings *against which* we act when impelled to do so by other stronger motives. These caveats must be borne in mind, whatever the views expressed in surveys. Be that as it may, most Moslems in France, when asked, say that they wish to be accepted as full members of the nation: and surely they would not say that if they accepted the Islamist demand that their Islamic identity is all that should matter to them? It is implausible to suggest that all who answer in this fashion are indulging in *taqqiyah*, the religiously permitted form of dissembling, particularly endorsed by Shia Muslims in times and places when they were persecuted, in order to further religious ends.

Westernization is in fact far advanced among Moslems in Europe, as elsewhere. This is evident from the Islamic marriage websites, for example. The men appear in western dress, as do the great majority of the women. What is striking about the websites for British Moslems, in fact, is that all the men look profoundly American, usually in t-shirts and often in baseball caps. Furthermore, the language in which they describe themselves is Mid-Atlantic, not British, English. They are fluent in psychobabble, that peculiar language that allows people to talk about themselves at considerable length without revealing anything, and which is a symptom of self-obsession unaccompanied by self-examination. Here is a young man who introduces himself by saying "Salaamz all," an expression redolent of cultural mixing if not of outright confusion, and who is looking for a Moslem woman to marry:

> I'm a laid back and relaxed individual. I am quite sarcastic and have a unique sense of humour. I can be childish at times but know when to be serious. I believe we all have our ups n downs but we should try to look for the good in ppl . . . I like going on long drives . . . keepin abreast of world affairs. I enjoy goin out for meals, goin to the cinema, bowling, snooker, cricket.

Asked to describe the level of their religious belief, all the searchers for brides or grooms say that they are "somewhat" religious, which suggests—at least to me—a level of commitment a good deal short of fanaticism. The young man above says of himself that "I am far from being able to call myself a perfect Muslim, but can say im [*sic*, and incidentally typical of the orthography of cellphone generations] a good human being." He says that he tries to pray, which means I suspect that he rarely succeeds, and that he "is working on becoming a 5 timer" (i.e., someone who prays five times a day). Now in my experience, people who say that they are "working on" something, such as a bad habit, a vile temper, eating too much, a sedentary lifestyle, laziness, giving up smoking, and so forth, rarely get anywhere because their heart is not in it. I would not, therefore, expect this young man to become a deeply observant Moslem in the near future, and I don't think he expects to either. He reiterates that he has a lot of room for improvement in his observance, but "I have a good heart and my intentions are clean," thus accepting the modern view, not by any means unique to Moslems, that, morally speaking, intention trumps both performance and effect (if he didn't believe it, and thought that others didn't believe it, he would hardly mention a trait that is clearly intended to be endearing rather than off-putting, a form of boasting dressed up as modesty).

FUN-LOVING MOSLEM WOMEN

Perhaps what the women write is more surprising, in view of the position of women often observed in Islamic societies. Here is what one woman, dressed in western clothes and with a photograph that shows her without a veil or a scarf, says (not untypically for the site) of herself:

> Hello all im a fun loving woman. im down to earth and do not judge people.

The idea that an unwillingness to pass judgment on people is a sign of moral election, and therefore a deeply attractive quality, is surely one that is much more compatible with and derived from secularism as it has developed in the western world in the last two or three decades, than it is compatible with or derives from Islam, especially in its fundamentalist mode.[19] Bear in mind that this woman is hoping to find a husband by her self-description, whom she supposes will share her self-congratulatory view (a very shallow one) of the proper role of the judgment of others in human life. In other words, she supposes that this view of the role of judgment—that is to say, none—is one held by many others. And one might remark in passing that "a sense of fun" is hardly one of the most obvious features of Islamic fundamentalists, though no doubt there are certain sour satisfactions to be derived from contemplating the fathomless depravity of all those who do not submit themselves unquestioningly to one's strictures.

The fun-loving woman goes on to say, "I am looking for a partner to settle down with." What is notable here is that, like any educated or semi-educated middle-class person who wants to demonstrate the modernity of his or her views, and their supposed enlightenment by comparison with the benightedness of the past, she strenuously avoids the use of the word "husband," with all its supposed connotations of subordination and obedience, preferring the politically correct, and utterly secular, word "partner." A partner is an equal, a 50 percent shareholder: a view of marriage that is completely irreligious.

Compared with the people who appear on marriage websites for evangelical Christians, the Muslims on the Islamic marriage websites are much less concerned with their religion: though, of course, all the Christians, like all the Moslems, have a good sense of humor. (Would anyone advertise himself as humorless? That, indeed, would be funny.) The religiosity of the Christians by comparison with the Moslems is perhaps not surprising: they, after

---

19. I am no expert, but I have not observed that fundamentalist Moslems experience much difficulty in passing judgment upon people.

all, have chosen to be religious in the midst of a society that is highly irreligious, and that tends to be condescending, at least in its intellectual portion, to religion. The Moslems, by contrast, though they are highly secularized *de facto*, emerge from a society in which to be totally and openly irreligious is almost unthinkable. It is the genius of Islam that it early found a method of binding people to itself once and for all, of never letting them go once they had adhered to it; it is by far the most enduring of politico-religious ideologies that has yet been devised. Even where the penalty for outright apostasy is not death, the social penalties applied to apostates such as ostracism are sufficiently strong that only fanatics of abstract truth are willing to suffer them. The great majority of humanity everywhere is unwilling to risk much for philosophical principles. This means that there will remain outward adherence even by the fun-loving and humorous Moslems, who will never go to the trouble of exposing their skepticism or incipient unbelief. Why bother, when the alternative is an easy life, lived high in the regard of others? Hypocrisy and dissimulation are what keeps social systems strong; it is intellectual honesty that destroys them.

FUNDAMENTALLY WRONG

The idea that the Moslem populations of Europe are seething with fanaticism or religious fundamentalism seems to me to be quite wrong.[20] This is not necessarily as comforting as might be supposed, however. First, there exist forms of Islam that undoubtedly do claim to provide all the answers to life's little problems, and discontented but intelligent adolescents are often

---

20. Even those surveys that show that up to 40 percent of young British Moslems claim that they want to live under Sharia law don't really worry me too much. An interesting follow-up question would be to ask them to describe those provisions of Sharia law that they would like to see instituted. I suspect that the answers would be vague. Certainly they do not make any efforts to emigrate to countries in which Sharia is incorporated into the law of the land. The attractions of the West are far too strong for that.

on the lookout for precisely such intellectual quack nostrums to resolve and overcome their adolescent angst or *Weltschmerz*. Second, an atmosphere in which Islam, even when lightly and hypocritically worn, cannot be repudiated *in toto* for fear of the social consequences is not one in which people can easily repudiate fanatics, one of whose claims is always to be more-Islamic-than-thou. This claim, incidentally, is the easier to make the laxer become the observances of the majority of the Moslems: I suspect it really is not very difficult to be more Islamic than the young man from whose marriage advertisement I have quoted. In the absence of a total and acknowledged rejection of Islam, therefore, on the grounds that it is based upon what is manifestly untrue, even such a fun-loving, cricket-playing young man with his unique sense of humor, who forgets to pray nineteen times out of twenty, will respect or sympathize with, even if he does not join, the fanatics and fundamentalists. Moreover, libertinism of the kind in which young Moslem men often indulge in Britain (a sure sign of their partial acculturation), sometimes leads to a sudden conversion to religious rigor. When you look into the history of Islamic religious fanatics in the West, they have often gone through a stage of debauchery, as indeed have Christian puritans. Life for them is one of those strange diagrams or pictures devised by psychologists that can be seen either as two crones facing one another, or two candlesticks, but not as both at the same time. For these people, life is either total self-indulgence or total self-denial: the concept of *l'homme moyen sensuel* is utterly alien to them, because the concept does not give them the intellectual certainty that they are looking for, always requiring as it does the play of judgment, which is precisely the quality that they do not have.

So while the number of fanatics is low and likely to remain so, the soil is propitious for their growth and sustenance; and even a few hundred fanatics (not a large number, after all) can sow a lot of chaos and cause a lot of death. It would be far better, of course, if there were no fanatics at all, but, while a terrible nuisance, they are unlikely to pose a fundamental threat to European societies unless those societies let them do so.[21] Such terrorist threats have been faced many times before in Europe, however, and there is no reason to suppose that this one is so formidable as to be insuperable.

Recently, while walking in the center of Birmingham, a once industrial British city with a large Moslem population, predominantly of Pakistani origin, I witnessed the behavior of a group of about ten young Moslem men as they walked along. They were dressed in the international slum-costume of the American ghetto; in imitation of the predominant local culture—I use the term in its strictly anthropological sense, all artefacts, regardless of value, being manifestations of a culture—several of them were tattooed, though their skins were singularly ill-adapted to this savage and stupid form of adornment or self-mutilation. Some of them had gold inlays in their front teeth, that infallible sign of gangster dentistry. They walked with the vulpine lope of young men who imagine that to be feared is to be respected. One of them had an apparatus that purveyed rap music compulsorily to passers-by; and their conversation, if a series of brief, solipsistic, shouted remarks can be called a conversation, was so larded with the word "fuck" and its various derivatives that no other words

---

21. In fact, the Archbishop of Canterbury, who—unlike Pope Benedict XVI—mistakes cowardice for bravery, surrender for victory, and platitudes for insights, is far more of a danger to Britain than Islamic fundamentalism on its own could ever be. He is, of course, the finest flower, if I may so put it, of an entire intellectual and social tendency. Another danger to British society is the use of the threat of Islamist terrorism by the government to increase its surveillance in other directions and for purposes other than to root out such terrorism. When a leading member of the opposition Conservative Party was arrested and questioned for nine hours by the police, his love letters to his wife having in the meantime been read by those connoisseurs of erotic literature, the Metropolitan Police, the justification for this outrage was an anti-terrorist law. If the police genuinely thought that the opposition politician, a Member of Parliament, was a terrorist threat, they should have been instantly dismissed from the service and admitted compulsorily to a mental hospital. Not he, but they sowed fear; and since it is intrinsically unlikely that policemen go round arresting senior politicians in a country like Britain without the connivance or say-so of other senior politicians, one is forced to the conclusion that those politicians who connived at his arrest wanted to sow fear in the hearts of those who opposed them. Incidentally, but not coincidentally, the politician who was arrested had uncovered disturbing evidence of government lying.

were audible, to me at least.[22] Furthermore, their demeanor—
loud and aggressive—was such as to intimidate: just you dare to
tell us to be quiet and behave ourselves!

Whatever else might be said of this charming scene, its roots
were not Islamic, but rather lay in the slum subculture that few
in authority now dare criticize for fear of being branded as elitist
or narrow-minded by members of the elite, or perhaps for purely
electoral reasons: but at any rate for reasons that indicate moral
cowardice clearly enough.

If the roots of their public conduct on the street I have described
are not Islamic, and it seems intrinsically unlikely that it is derived
from any religious tradition whatever, that does not mean that
the young men are culturally indistinguishable from others in the
larger society. They are acculturated, perhaps, to the worst aspects
of modern British urban life, but not therefore integrated; they
retain a specificity that is Islamic, or at least of a culture that is
deeply marked by Islam.

Such groups as the one I saw on a street in the city center of
Birmingham are never mixed racially. Only very rarely do they
include women, and when they do the women are not dressed in
American ghetto costume, but usually in black and with at least a
headscarf to preserve their modesty. Degeneracy is for men, not
for women.

The young men of the type who form these groups are not
deeply religious; when they end up in prison, as they increasingly
often do,[23] they express no interest in the imam's visits, they do

---

22. Oddly enough, the young Moslems of Birmingham, unlike those of other British cities,
have developed an accent of their own, which is related to, but quite distinguishable from,
the native local accent. While I understand that *de gustibus non est disputandum*, and all
that, the fact is that it is hideously ugly without the compensatory advantages of inventive
expressiveness.

23. Young Moslem males are four times over-represented in British prisons by comparison
with their proportion in the general population. This is unlikely to be a consequence of
racism, since Hindus and Sikhs are under-represented in them. In France, upwards of
60 percent of prisoners are Moslem. This is not quite as dramatic as may be supposed,
because (so it is sometimes claimed) a quarter of all French young men of the age group
most likely to be imprisoned are Moslem. It should be borne in mind also that the French
rate of imprisonment is slightly less that that in Britain. Another interesting fact, which
also argues against racism being an important determinant of a person's fate in Britain,

not pray five times a day or even once, they do not keep Ramadan except if they have to make a court appearance, in which case the supposed weakness induced by the daily fast is brought forward as a pretext not to attend, and they do not even demand halal food.[24] Their general manner is not such as one might expect of religious Moslems, gravity being the last word one would use to describe it.

These young men are nevertheless extremely anxious to preserve what they call the honor of their women, their sisters in particular, whose "honor" they will protect with machetes and even, if need be, by means of murder, including of their sisters themselves. In doing so, they resort to supposedly religious justifications and sanctions for what in reality amounts to the crude domination of women.

THE WOMAN QUESTION

Before I go any further, let me add that I am not claiming that the treatment of women by other groups is always impeccable, far from it. As the formal structure of relations between men and women has broken down (here I am speaking in particular of Britain), consequent upon the utopian belief long peddled by intellectuals that if only relations between the sexes could be placed on a "natural" rather than a conventional basis, that is to say according to mutual affection alone rather than to contract, social pressure, mutual obligation, sense of duty, etc., then—and only then—would the full beauty of the human personality flourish, as well as the full enjoyment of human sexuality. In the

---

is that, while the unemployment rate of young Moslems is considerably higher than the national average, that of the Hindus and Sikhs is somewhat lower. The role of Islam in producing this result is not necessarily straightforward, of course. For example, the Moslems and Hindus might have emerged from different social classes of society in the first place. But unless Moslems are (wrongly) conceived of as a race apart, racism cannot be the explanation.

24. The same has been found in French prisons. See *L'islam dans les prisons*, Farhad Khosrokhavar, Balland, Paris, 2004.

event, unfortunately, promiscuity increased while the desire for the exclusive sexual possession of another did not in any degree abate, leading not surprisingly to an access of jealousy which, equally unfortunately, is the most powerful instigator of violence between the sexes. It also instigates violence between young men, especially between those young men whose social status is dependent entirely upon the possession of a woman (or women), their status in all other respects being lowly because their accomplishments and economic prospects are lowly. A sexually predatory man in a sexually predatory environment is naturally inclined to believe that he, or his "partner," is being preyed upon, and he thereby insulted and made to look a fool. Marriage may be dead,[25] but the fear of cuckoldry is stronger than ever.

There is a difference between the Islamic and non-Islamic form of mistreatment of women, however. The latter is purely egoistic, while the former, while egoistic in origin also, claims to have a justification in a wider social and religious morality. I leave it to

---

25. Forty-two percent of births in Britain (and rising) are now out of what used to be called wedlock, and while a quarter of marriages break down within ten years, leaving the children to cope with the divorce as best they can, the rate of break-up of non-married relationships is considerably higher. It is established beyond reasonable doubt that step-parenthood is statistically associated with the abuse of children, both physical and sexual, and while it might be argued that the relationship is not therefore proved to be causative, because statistical association can arise for reasons other than causation, the fact that the wicked step-parent is an ancient one in literature suggests that step-parenthood does cause otherwise avoidable abuse. In the area in which I worked as a doctor in Britain, to ask a young person who his or her father was had become indelicate, because it was felt to imply an unfavorable moral judgment. Were it not for the presence of Indian immigrants and their descendents, the illegitimacy rate in that area would have been virtually 100 percent. When I asked one adolescent girl who her father was, she replied, "Do you mean my father at the moment?" I have been called "Dad" by more than one child, presumably because he thought that all males were potentially his father. This seemed to be taking the principles of "it takes a village" to extremes.

It is odd, moreover, that homosexuals should insist on the right to marry at precisely the time when the prestige of marriage as an institution should be at its lowest ebb in the eyes of the general population. Likewise, it is odd that so much technological effort (and brilliance) should go into assisting the fertility of the infertile at precisely the time when women are more reluctant to bear children than at any time in history (with the possible exception of the Indians of Mexico and Peru after the Spanish Conquest). I suppose that a general wilfulness, a refusal to accept fate in the slightest degree, and a corresponding desire to mold life according to one's wishes, unites these phenomena.

philosophers to work out which is worse, from the point of view of moral philosophy; I am content for the moment to remark the difference.

There are two other lines of evidence regarding the hold on Islam, or pseudo-Islam, on these young men. The first is that they joyfully join in the mass debauchery to be witnessed everywhere in Britain at the weekends, though they rigidly exclude their sisters from joining in; therefore they have no principled objection to mass debauchery as such. They regard young white women in Britain, not without good reason, as vulgar sluts,[26] often openly and publicly calling them sluts, *ex officio* as it were, when they venture into the predominantly Moslem areas of a city, and keeping one or more of them in a state of contemptuous concubinage after their own marriages to a girl deemed suitable for them by their parents.

The second line of evidence arises from the different response of young Moslem men and women to the marriages that are arranged for them by their parents, and forced upon them if they are unwilling. As a doctor, I saw over the years scores and perhaps even hundreds of young women who had made a suicidal gesture because of such a forced marriage; in the same period, I saw only one young man make a similar gesture.

The young man or woman would be taken "home" to the village from which the parents had emigrated, and there told that he or she was to marry a first cousin, sometimes illiterate and rarely fluent in English. All of them knew of cases in which defiance of the parents' wishes had ended in virtual imprisonment, violence, and even death, and such cases had acted as the execution of Admiral Byng did, according to Voltaire: *pour encourager les autres.* But what was tolerable and even desirable for the young men, was intolerable and repugnant to the young women. The young men got a domestic slave and sexual servant, while being free to lead a western life away from home; the young women, by contrast, became the domestic slave and sexual servant of a man

---

26. One sixteen-year-old said to me "My mother calls me a slut, but I'm good at what I do."

whom they might regard as a peasant boor, at whose touch they shuddered.[27]

The importance of male domination of women for maintaining a vaguely Islamic sentiment among young men (that seems to me to have little religious about it) is illustrated by the following anecdote about the prison in which I worked. A young Moslem, imprisoned for a relatively minor crime, came to me complaining about abdominal pain, but it soon became evident to me that something else was bothering him. I asked him what it was and before long he told me.

Not long before he had given evidence for the prosecution in a murder trial. Two men, the father and brother of the deceased, had killed a young woman because she refused to go along with the marriage laid down for her, in order to preserve the "honor" of the family. The father and brother of the young woman were found guilty and duly sentenced. The young prisoner who had complained of abdominal pain was now under threat from other Moslem prisoners, including those unrelated to the family, for his supposed treachery. They had made it clear that they were going to get him for it, and he was frightened for his life. I arranged for him to be sent to another prison forthwith.

The feeling against him was not that of prisoners against informers in general. Prisoners draw the line at murder and generally do not cover up for murderers, except out of fear. No, this young man's testimony in court was regarded as treachery because it threatened the whole system of relations between men and women, a system as highly convenient to the young men of

---

27. The high rate of consanguinity in marriages leads, unsurprisingly, to a high rate of otherwise rare genetic diseases, until recently a taboo subject in the medical and other press. I also observed a curious syndrome, if a mere pattern of behavior may be called a syndrome, that does little credit to human nature. It was not common but it definitely occurred. The husband of the forced marriage would arrive in Britain on a temporary permit. In the first year, according to the regulations, the wife could object to his presence in the country and he would have to return to Pakistan. After a year of good behavior, however, he was entitled to and received a permanent leave to stay. The very day following receipt of this permanent leave, his violent abuse of his wife would begin, perhaps worsened by a desire for revenge upon her humiliation of him in having in effect emasculated him for a year.

the type who ended up in prison as it was agonizing to the women who suffered it.[28]

Another anecdote, told me by the dean of a medical school, illustrates the hold of men over women that male Moslems in Britain (and France and Holland) want to preserve, and that in my view reinforces their wish for a separate, quasi-religious identity. A group of four female Moslem medical students suddenly started to appear on the wards dressed in the niqab, that tent-like form of dress that allows women only a slit for the eyes. This alarmed the medical school authorities, and it is no doubt a sign of their complete lack of confidence, personal or cultural, that they felt unable, on their own authority alone, to forbid the adoption of this costume by female medical students: for had they done so, they would have laid themselves open to the most fearsome of all charges, that of discrimination.

Fortunately, the authorities were able to find a regulation dating back to 1857, before there was any question of the niqab in British medical schools, which required that any doctor, or doctor in training, must show his face to the person he was examining (indeed, a very sensible requirement). The dean was therefore able to tell the medical students that they had either to remove their niqab or leave the medical school. They duly did the former; and, interestingly, they returned to the dean a couple of weeks later and informed him that they had never wanted to wear them in the first place. They had been bullied and blackmailed into doing so by male fundamentalist students—who, of course, wore western dress.

---

28. You might have supposed that the feminists would have been militant in their opposition to the system, which leads in many cases to a misery greater than any I have witnessed outside catastrophic civil war, but you would be wrong. Instead, hardly a peep has been heard from them. There are no doubt three reasons for the existence of what Sherlock Holmes would no doubt have called the feminists who did not protest. The first is physical cowardice; the second moral cowardice, in that they would face accusations of racism, etc. if they protested; the third that they would have to give up the multiculturalism which, as radical opponents of anything smacking of tradition, they usually believe in also. An honorable exception to my strictures is the liberal commentator Polly Toynbee, with whom I am usually not in agreement, to put it mildly; but she had the honesty to acknowledge the contradiction between feminism and multiculturalism, and chose to hang on to the former at the expense of the latter.

But how, you might ask, were such female medical students so easily blackmailed? The answer is that the young men would have informed their parents (liberal in the context) that their daughters were behaving in a promiscuous way. This would have been quite sufficient for their parents to withdraw them from medical school. Suffice it to say that no such argument would be sufficient to persuade Moslem parents to withdraw their sons from medical school. Nor, of course, did the blackmailing students truly believe that the niqab was a religious requirement; if they had, after all, they would have insisted that the female students leave the medical school rather than abandon it. The whole episode was an exertion of male domination.

It might be argued, of course, that such domination is not unique, either historically or anthropologically, to Islamic societies, and there is undoubtedly truth in this argument. Even forced marriage is not unique to them: Capulet in *Romeo and Juliet* tries to force an unwanted marriage on to Juliet and threatens to disown her completely and for ever if she does not comply with his wishes. Forced marriage also makes it appearance in *A Midsummer Night's Dream,* so the concept can hardly have been an alien one to Elizabethan audiences. The list of legal disabilities under which women in the West have labored in the past, sometimes the recent past, would be a long one, and we forget our own history if we suppose that the current state of equality between the sexes has been a perennial or immemorial one.

VIVE LA DIFFÉRENCE

And yet there is undoubtedly something in Islamic societies (at least until they attempt to secularize) in point of the radical inequality of the sexes that is profoundly different from western societies as they have developed. Whether western and Islamic societies were always different in their attitude to women is beside the point; they are very different now. It is surely not a coincidence that 87 percent of European converts to Islam are men; I do not have the figures for Christian converts, or for "born again"

Christians, but I should be very surprised if they were the same. And, however accurate or otherwise that last statement may be, what is indisputable is that the nature of the argument or discussion within Islam about the requirement or mere advisability of wearing the niqab takes us back to an entirely pre-Enlightenment, indeed pre-Reformation, mode of thought. Here is argumentation quite untouched by the spirit of the famous motto of the Royal Society (one of the most ancient scientific societies in the world, with perhaps the most distinguished history): *Nullius in verba*, on the word—that is to say the authority—of no one. Evidence is henceforth the supreme authority. By contrast, everything on the question of the niqab, as in all other disputes on what consitutes "correct" Islamic law, custom, and behavior, is on the word of someone. All argument derives from an unquestionable authority, which is worshipped with all the devotion that a fetishist lavishes upon his fetish; everything turns upon the supposedly correct interpretation of texts, more than a thousand years old, be it of the Koran itself or of the collections of supposedly authentic Hadith. Whether women must, ought, or need not wear the niqab is a question upon which the last millennium of human development can, even in principle, shed no light at all, nor can any evidence derived from anything other than the internal evidence of the fetishistic texts. Here is a fairly typical example of the method of argumentation that in Moslem religious circles is taken as being adequate not only to the settling of this question, but the settling of all questions (the author does not think that the wearing of the niqab is religiously required, but that it is nevertheless religiously meritorious to do so):

> Even after Surah an-Nur ayah 31 had been revealed, ordinary
> Muslim women continued to wear niqab with the approval of the
> Prophet (sAas). This has specifically been mentioned for Umm
> Khallad (Sunan Abu Dawud Book 14 #2482), Asma bint Abu
> Bakr (Muwatta Book 20 #20.5.16), and some Qurayshi women
> who were visiting the Prophet (sAas) (Sahih Bukhari Book 54
> #515). As well, the fact that the Prophet (sAas) had to tell women
> not to wear niqab and gloves in ihram (Sahih Bukhari Book 29

#64) means that niqab and gloves were well-known and worn by a substantial number of sahabiyat (rAa). Clearly this form of extra modesty has the approval of the Prophet (sAas) and that is another reason that it is sunna.

Of course, writers can be found who come to a different conclusion from the texts, using different little bits to come to what is probably their pre-ordained conclusion: that the niqab is religiously compulsory. But their methods are essentially the same: they sift the texts as Roman priests sifted the entrails of slaughtered chickens for auguries as to how to behave. The method gives rise to considerable dialectical refinement (as it did and does with Talmudic scholars, and perhaps with lawyers of the Anglo-American Common Law); but it is stifles originality, is wasteful of human intelligence, and is intellectually claustrophobic. Just as the Jews were able to make their remarkably disproportionate contributions to modern intellectual and cultural life only when substantially freed of their Talmudic Judaism (which, however, prepared them intellectually to make those contributions), so Moslems will not make many valuable contributions to intellectual or cultural life until their brightest people turn their intelligence to something other than supposed exegesis of supposedly infallible texts. No doubt liberation is made more difficult by the examples both of Christianity and Judaism that religious Moslems have before them: for it is clear that, once intelligence is turned to something other than scholasticism, religion ceases to be much of a living force in society.[29]

Be that as it may, the situation of Moslem women in Britain, and elsewhere in Europe, has led to a seeming paradox (I hope I shall be forgiven for generalizing in a way that cannot possibly be accurate in every case), though the paradox is only a seeming one. The young women in these circumstances are superior in every way to their male contemporaries, despite their disadvantages (again, one is tempted to say because of, rather than despite, them). They are better-spoken, appear vastly more intelligent, and

---

29. The nominal Christianity of most Americans notwithstanding.

are as charming as the males are charmless, having been born and raised without that sense of entitlement which only a corresponding sense of *noblesse oblige* can render tolerable, and which is entirely absent in this case.

If I were an employer, I should favor them very strongly as employees because work for them is a liberation rather than an unfortunate and even unjust intrusion between periods of amusement. They are eager, even desperate to learn; money is not their only or even their principle motive for working.

Another seeming paradox is this: that often, despite (and yet again one is tempted to say because of) the fact that they have been illegally kept away from school since the age of twelve, either at home or sent away to molder in rural Pakistan, they remain better educated, more literate, and more numerate, than either their brothers or their white working-class female contemporaries who have received at least four years more schooling. This is because, on the one hand, their brothers feel that they have achieved something, perhaps all that they ever need to achieve, by having been born male when they could so easily have been born female,[30] while they, the sisters, appreciate early on that education is a possible route to personal salvation in this life. Moreover, the very submissiveness inculcated in them at home is conducive to learning as much as possible at school. On the other hand, they remain superior to white working-class girls because the latter inhabit a social world that is not merely indifferent, but actively hostile, to education and the exercise of intelligence. For them, extra years of schooling actually decrease the sum total of their knowledge, while they increase their attraction to social pathology.

The situation of these young women is truly tragic. They are sufficiently influenced by western culture to reject, indeed find abhorrent, the destiny marked out for them by the culture which their mothers, knowing no other, unselfconsciously accepted; but yet they are not fully integrated, either, into western society. They live in a cultural no man's land, and their situation is made all

---

30. Like many people born lucky, they attribute their good fortune to pre-existing virtue; and so their good luck is only a due reward or what they are entitled to.

the more difficult by the fact that their parents, far from being neglectful (or worse) as are those of so many white girls, are loving and anxious to do the right thing for their daughters as they see it. They are thus faced with a tragic dilemma: do what their parents want, and live a life that is abhorrent to them ever afterwards; or disobey their parents and alienate, perhaps forever, those who gave them life and to whom they have been socialized into believing that they have deep and inescapable obligations.

Their situation is not made better by the attitude (if indifference can properly be called an attitude) to their fate of the society into which their parents immigrated. I have already mentioned the silence of feminists about their suffering. Angered by the use of the use of words such as "chairman" rather than "chair" or "chairperson," they maintain a studious silence about the way that young women in the situation I have described are often regarded, or even treated, as prostitutes by their own "community" if they disobey their parents or leave an abusive husband, or if a husband leaves them because (for example) she has borne him two seriously malformed children—the consequence of consanguinity—for which he naturally, and rightfully in the eyes of the "community," blames her.

Informal indifference, such as that of the feminists, is one thing, perhaps; but official indifference is another. Many of my young female Moslem patients described how they were illegally kept away from school by their parents, especially from the age of twelve. Not a single one, however, ever described any efforts by school inspectors to return them to school, as it was the statutory duty of the inspectors to do—and to prosecute parents who refused to send their children to school unless they were educating them formally at home.

No male child was ever kept away from school in this fashion.

The school inspectors were certainly not totally inactive. Official idleness was not sufficient to explain their inactivity in the cases of young Moslem girls absent from school. I recall the case of a white working-class stepfather who was driven to a suicide attempt by the relentless pursuit of the school inspectors, who were now threatening to prosecute him, because his fifteen-year-old step-daughter, who was utterly beyond his control, repeatedly truanted from school. This man had done everything he reasonably could to get her to attend; he delivered her to school personally whenever she consented to be driven there by him (though, of course, she was only too aware that he could not take her there physically against her will, for fear of being accused by her of assault). Despite the most obvious fact that even if she attended school she would learn nothing because she was determined to learn nothing, and would almost certainly so disrupt proceedings in the school as to prevent others from learning anything, if there were children there of a mind to learn, the school inspectors persisted in persecuting him as if the whole future of the country depended upon his stepdaughter's attendance at school. This would have been cruelly absurd at the best of times; but there is something deeply sinister in the contrast with the complete inactivity of the same inspectors in the face of an entire and much more significant social phenomenon.

Here, it seems to me, we get a glimpse of the sickness that pervades Europe.

4.

SUMMARY AND CONCLUSIONS SO FAR

Europe shows signs of demographic decline, with some the lowest fertility rates ever recorded, all the more remarkable as they have come about without any state intervention enforcing them (unlike, for example, the Chinese one-child policy). They are a reflection of the people's wishes, at least under present conditions. We will enquire later as to why these should be the people's wishes.

The aging of the population, however, is not necessarily as disastrous as is sometimes suggested. Societies and mankind in general are very adaptable; new situations call forth new solutions. It is mistaken to think of a person as necessarily a drain on society merely because he has reached a certain age.

Immigration into Europe causes fear and despondency because immigrants threaten to overwhelm the local culture and change it to their own. No doubt this could happen, given sufficient numbers and a sufficiently pusillanimous response by the host society; but it is unlikely. The apocalyptic view is mistaken because it assumes a uniformity of opinion and interest among Moslems that does not exist, though it is conceivable that it could be created. The cause of pusillanimity is another question we shall look into.

It is, of course, easy enough to find tenets of Islam and interpretations of such tenets that make it completely incompatible with a free society. Perhaps the most important example is the penalty of death for apostates, endorsed (I believe) by all four major schools of Sunni jurisprudence, though there is some dissension. I am far from being anti-religious, even though I have no religious belief myself; but this tenet seems to me to be quite beyond the pale of civilized discourse in the twenty-first century. While it is no doubt efficacious in controlling and suppressing religious dissent in countries such as Afghanistan and Bangladesh, nothing can detract from its primitive savagery.

But, intolerant of apostasy as many Moslems undoubtedly are, very few really wish to kill apostates, and the few that do are dangerous only if we allow them to be dangerous (in other words, the danger is both in them and in us). If, for example, we show ourselves so intimidated by a few treacherous mullahs in Denmark that Mohammed and his legacy can no longer be mocked, derided, excoriated, or rationally criticized in public, and pass laws to preserve sensitive bigots from hurt feelings, we have only ourselves to blame if the most extreme and retrograde forms of the religion triumph in the minds of the young and impressionable.[31]

---

31. President Bush's response was particularly feeble and cowardly, and belied his reputation for belligerence. In fact, the founding moment, so to speak, of western pusillanimity probably occurred more than a decade earlier, in the wake of the Ayatollah Khomeini's fatwa against the author Salman Rushdie for his book *The Satanic Verses*. One Moslem notable in Britain, Iqbal Sacranie, later knighted for his services to moderation, said of the gangster-like fatwa that it was wrong because "it is a bit too easy for him, his mind must be tormented for the rest of his life unless he asks for forgiveness to Almighty Allah." This is not a point of view likely to deter many assassins. Other Moslem leaders in Britain (always self-proclaimed; it is one of the strengths and weaknesses of Islam that, having no indisputable hierarchy, whoever proclaims himself leader today can be outflanked by someone tomorrow) said that the fatwa was wrong because it misinterpreted Islamic law, but never because it was contrary to *British* law, let alone because it was wrong in itself to call for the death of a writer. Yet others, notoriously, called openly for Rushdie's death with placards. The then-secretary of the Bradford Council of Mosques said that Rushdie had tortured Islam and deserved to be hanged. He added that he would himself be prepared to kill Rushdie, and would willingly sacrifice his own life and that of his children to do so. Nor was he alone; the vice-chairman (n.b. not vice-chair or vice-chairperson) said that retribution against Rushdie was justified, as it was against anyone involved in the publication of the book. The Islamist intellectual Dr. Kalim Saddiqui, who wanted to create an Islamic

state within the British state, told a meeting that "I would like every Moslem to raise his hand in agreement with the death sentence on Salman Rushdie. Let the world see that every Moslem agrees that this man should be put away."

These statements and declarations were made in a context in which the threat to the author was a very serious practical possibility, and not merely a lot of rhetorical hot air. An Iranian blew himself up in London in an attempt to kill Salman Rushdie (it is indeed fortunate that Moslem terrorists are so often incompetent, although this is by no means always to be relied upon). There is no reason to think that the statements and declarations above were meant rhetorically or metaphorically. Furthermore, demonstrators unambiguously called for the death of the author, and not in the way that literary theorists mean it. They held up placards in public saying "Kill Rushdie." Yet not a single prosecution was brought against anyone, notwithstanding the following provision of the Offences Against the Persons Act (1861): "whosoever shall solicit, encourage, persuade, or endeavour to persuade, or shall propose to any person, to murder any other person, whether he be a subject of Her Majesty or not, and whether he be within the Queen's dominions or not, shall be guilty of a misdemeanor, and being convicted thereof shall be liable to [imprisonment for life]."

In explaining its unutterable cowardice to Parliament, the government—then headed by the supposedly redoubtable Mrs. Thatcher—argued that there was insufficient evidence to bring a prosecution, even though the statute is pretty clear, and the words "Kill Rushdie" are not very difficult to construe. The response of quite a number of British intellectuals, across the spectrum from Hugh Trevor-Roper to Germaine Greer, was of a similar degree of cowardice. Many of them animadverted, in a giggly way, on the author's supposedly unpleasant character, as if the whole business were merely a spat between two lovers, Trevor-Roper for example saying he wouldn't mind if some Islamists took Rushdie down a dark alley and instilled some manners into him by means of a beating. That Trevor-Roper and the others—who, after all, could have maintained their silence on the matter—were acting from cowardice is made plain by the following thought experiment. Suppose that a wild Christian fundamentalist cleric had called for the death of an author who had suggested that Christ was a homosexual: does anyone think that Trevor-Roper *et al.* would have sallied forth to support, or at least to "understand," the cleric? The difference is surely this, and only this: that when Moslem clerics call for someone's death, they are to be taken seriously. If a Christian cleric called for someone's death he would be publicly excoriated, but privately derided, because, despite much huffing and puffing and righteous indignation, no one would believe that he really meant what he said.

It is true that, in bringing prosecutions, not only the fact of the commission of an offense and the likelihood of a successful court outcome has to be borne in mind, but the public interest in securing a conviction also. The government of the day clearly took the view that it did not want to stir up trouble among the Moslem population, particularly of Bradford which seemed particularly exercised about a book that it had not read and did not want anyone else to read. All governments want, if possible, to avoid unrest and promote social cohesion, but what serves to do this in the short term may not serve to do it in the long.

There is reason to think that, in this case, cowardice was expedient, but courage would have been wise. To have prosecuted and punished rigorously, even at the cost of some temporary inconvenience such as a riot or two, would have sent a clear and unambiguous message that western society was determined to defend its freedoms against thuggish obscurantism (the fact that, to many, Rushdie was an unattractive figure would only have strengthened the message). Instead, for the sake a night's peace, the government chose appeasement, with disastrous effects throughout the world, and particularly for the Moslem population of Great Britain. The lesson was drawn that the West preferred its comfort to its principle, with the result that it was not able fully to preserve either. The appeasement was particularly disastrous for the Moslems of Great Britain because it demonstrated that those among them who did not approve of murdering authors and the like could expect no vigorous support from either the British intelligentsia or the British law, and therefore left no moral or intellectual counterweight to the Islamists within the Moslem population. Intimidation was seen to work; but intimidation is like corruption, according to the view of the latter of the late Marshal Sese Seko Mobutu (who knew a thing or two about it): it takes two to make it work. It is a shame that Mrs. Thatcher, who knew a lot of poetry by heart, did not let a few lines of Kipling's verse guide her in this instance:

> It is always a temptation to a rich and lazy nation
> To puff and look important and to say:
> "Though we know we should defeat you, we have not the time to meet you.
> We will therefore pay you cash to go away."

> And that is called paying the Dane-geld;
> But we've proved it again and again,
> That if once you have paid him the Dane-geld
> You never get rid of the Dane.

In the light of the policy that was actually followed, the last verse is not encouraging:

> "We never pay any one Dane-Geld,
> No matter how trifling the cost,
> For the end of that game is oppression and shame,
> And the nation that plays it is lost."

If the British government had shown a little spine during the Salman Rushdie affair, and if other western countries had realized how vitally important it was for them to stand together, I think it is possible (though not of course certain, because no counterfactual can be certain) that the world would have been saved a lot of trouble.

Since then, there have been a lot of small displays of spinelessness. One example is the odious and unctuous American Christmas greeting of "Happy Holidays," which seems to be prevalent in those parts of the United States with concentrations of intellectuals (a modern example of Julien Benda's famous *trahison des clercs*). I doubt very much whether any Moslem, Jew, Buddhist, Hindu, Confucian, Parsee, or animist has ever been offended by the greeting of Merry Christmas, and if he had he should have been told to go and boil his head. Compare this supposed sensitivity to the religious susceptibilities of others with the behavior of the staff of the Bangladeshi restaurant, owned and run entirely by Moslems in the little town in England where I live half the year, who shortly before Christmas put up decorations and handed out Christmas cards to all their customers wishing them a merry Christmas. Although I did not specifically ask, I have little doubt that the staff considered themselves good Moslems nonetheless. It is not difficult, however, to find websites on the internet condemning such tolerance as un-Islamic; and, by a curious transvaluation of all values, the ayatollahs of religious and cultural sensitivity would, by implication, agree with them. (Incidentally, the day after I ate at the restaurant I spoke to a Moslem employee of my bank whose last words to me as I rang off were, "Have a nice Christmas." I wished him the same, without calling curses down on my head.) There could be no clearer illustration of the fact that our problems with Islam are as much to do with ourselves as with Islam itself, which is not to say that there are no problems with Islam.

Again, why we are so easily intimidated physically and intellectually, by people whose weapons are primitive and whose intellectual resources are practically nil (not as individuals, I hasten to add, but as inheritors of a tradition that has been exhausted for hundreds of years), is a question that I shall seek to answer.

One modern trend often blamed for Europe's lack of cultural confidence is relativism, both philosophical and cultural. The transmission of what you have inherited, and the act of defending yourself against dangers, seems to require a belief in the worth of what is to be transmitted and defended: and relativism radically undermines that belief.

5.

THE ROLE OF RELATIVISM, MORAL AND EPISTEMOLOGICAL

All western philosophy, said the mathematician and philosopher Alfred North Whitehead, is footnotes to Plato. In other words, the fundamental questions of truth, knowledge, justice, goodness, and beauty were raised by Plato 2,400 years ago and have never been answered since, once and for all as it were, indisputably and to everyone's satisfaction. This in itself is a powerful argument for relativism: for if the questions were answerable, surely by now people—among them the most brilliant minds our species can boast—would have found the answers. Perhaps it is not altogether surprising that Whitehead also said, "There are no whole truths; all truths are half truths." (If all truths are half truths, is the truth that all truths are half truths a quarter truth, and so on *ad infinitum?*)

Perhaps Pontius Pilate was right after all, or at least not completely wrong, when he asked what truth was and would not stay for an answer.

COME BACK, DESCARTES, WE NEED YOU

The sources of relativism are two: abstract and empirical. If in principle you cannot found or ground any fact, or aesthetic or moral judgment, upon an indubitable, metaphysically certain premise that every rational being must accept and cannot but accept without falling into self-evident contradiction, then it follows that all facts and judgments are without secure foundation and therefore are vulnerable to criticism. In fact—that is, if there were such a thing as fact—no judgment is to be preferred to any other, at least not on merely evidential grounds. The choice between them is therefore arbitrary. From this it follows that what determines a man's belief, whether it refers either to fact or to moral or aesthetic judgment, can never be his honest assessment of the evidence for or against it. What counts is what he wants to believe; and what he wants to believe is in turn determined by his interests, material or psychological as the case may be.

Now of course, no man does, or indeed could, live as if epistemological relativism were true, or as if moral and aesthetic judgments were only expressions of personal preference or of a will to power. Not only is such radical skepticism psychologically impossible (no one would be able even so much as to make a cup of tea if he really made skepticism his lived reality), but it runs into more or less the same contradiction that Logical Positivism ran into. Logical Positivism claimed that statements were either empirically verifiable or tautologous (that is to say, true by definition of the terms in the subject and predicate) on the one hand, or meaningless on the other: mere gibberish that might, or might not, happen to have the form of grammatically correct sentences, but which referred to nothing outside itself, and inherently neither true nor false. The problem for Logical Positivism was that its own doctrine was neither empirically verifiable nor tautologous,

and therefore it was hoist on its own petard: if true, it was meaningless, and therefore, according to itself, neither true nor false.

Clearly the claim of the relativists is not a small one, tenta-
tively advanced by people who are deeply unsure of themselves.
They make statements that rely for their force on their absolute
truth. One school of relativists, for example, emphasizes the fact
that scientific theories are merely provisional to deny the claim
of science to be knowledge in the sense of justified, true belief,
or indeed to have any special status at all; and some go further
still, basing themselves upon the historic-philosophical work of
Thomas Kuhn, who argued that scientists change their theories
not according to evidence, or because the evidence demands it,
but for a variety of extraneous reasons, psychological, economic,
institutional, etc. And since there is always more than one theory
that can account for any phenomenon, the choice between them
is arbitrary, a matter more of taste than of truth. (The status of
Occam's Razor, which says, in effect, that theories should be
the simplest possible that can explain what is to be explained, is
ambiguous. It seems more like a chef's tip about how to cook well
than a rule of logic or a contingent truth about the world. After
all, why should the simplest theory always be the best? In medicine, doctors try to account for all the symptoms of a patient by
diagnosing a single illness that satisfactorily explains them, but
sometimes patients do have more than one illness, and this is so
irrespective of whether or not one diagnosis will explain all their
symptoms. Most doctors have been misled at some time in their
careers by the beauty and elegance of their theory about what is
wrong with a patient.)

THE ATTACK ON SCIENCE

This attack on science is important and significant for Europe
because Europe claims (I think correctly) to be the cradle of

science: that is to say, of a self-conscious interrogation of Nature by means of observation and experiment that leads to an accretion of knowledge about the workings of Nature. It is part of Europe's self-image that it introduced science into the world and therefore all the material benefits that flow from science: untune that string, and hark what discord follows. If science is in fact no different from shamanistic divination in its intellectual foundations, then Europe has contributed nothing distinctive or important to the world, in the same way that, if the claims of Islam are untrue, if the Koran is actually a compilation cobbled together for political reasons and not the revealed word of God, if the Hadith are historically bogus, if a large number of Islamic ceremonies are profoundly pagan in their origins, then Islam has contributed nothing of intellectual worth to the world for hundreds of years and the self-image of Moslems would be profoundly affected. (This, of course, gives us a clue as to what Islamic fundamentalism in the modern world is really all about.)

Kuhn's model of science, as being fundamentally irrational,[32] is based first upon a supposedly correct interpretation of scientific history, and secondly upon a very restricted view of the total field of science. For his strictures about the nature of science to be valid, his interpretation of history must be true, and true absolutely: there can be no skepticism there, or else the philosophical point he is trying to make fails completely.

Moreover, it is not true that scientific theories are always quite as provisional as sometimes claimed. The greatest single discovery, perhaps, in the history of physiology was William Har-

---

32. Or perhaps one should say arational, since on his account it is difficult to see what would or could count for the rational investigation of Nature. If no view is better than any other, no view is worse either. There have, of course, been other philosophical attacks on the "objectivity" of science, for example by Paul Feyerabend. Foucault suggested that, behind every human utterance, including the utterances of science, there was an unacknowledged lust for power. It does not follow from this that there is no such thing as truth: presumably every human act, including an utterance about science, is motivated by something. What that something might be is, potentially at least, an empirical question. No number of facts could prove that truth does not exist, for truth is a precondition of factuality. Moreover, it is obvious that the motive behind the utterance of a statement, while often interesting and even important to know, is not the same as the truth or untruth of that statement.

ENCOUNTER BOOKS

900 Broadway

New York, New York 10003-1239

www.encounterbooks.com
Please add me to your mailing list.

Name

Company

Address

City, State, Zip

E-mail

Book Title

vey's discovery of the circulation of the blood (it doesn't matter for my philosophical purposes, however, whether it was or was not the greatest single discovery). Does anyone seriously expect that a revision of this theory will ever be necessary, in the sense that a proof will be forthcoming that the blood does not, in fact, circulate? No doubt mathematical physicists might claim that Harvey was a mere naturalist rather than a true scientist, in so far as he did not reduce the circulation of the blood to mathematics; but there is no reason why mathematical physics should be considered the only truly scientific activity. Some things come to be known by experiment that are beyond reasonable doubt.

Thomas Kuhn's view of science was accepted for the kind of reasons he said that paradigm shifts occurred in science itself: that is to say, for reasons extraneous to the evidential merits of the new paradigm. In showing that science had epistemological feet of clay, Kuhn was appealing to those intellectuals who felt vaguely guilty that they knew nothing of science (why bother to go to the trouble of knowing anything of it, if it had not special claims to knowledge?), but at a deeper level he appealed to those western intellectuals who saw the self-denigration of the West in general, and of Europe in particular, the originator of science as a self-conscious activity, as the path to moral self-aggrandizement. The more thorough the self-denigration, the more generous, open, and liberal-minded the person.

Clearly, there was and still is something of Marie Antoinette playing shepherdess about this rejection of science. If people really thought there was nothing to choose between, say, witchcraft as practiced by African tribes and modern aeronautics, no one would ever get on an aircraft. It is true that millions of people in the West believe, or claim to believe, in the healing chakras of the earth, yin and yang, and the like, but only in two circumstances: when there is nothing much wrong with them other than a vague dissatisfaction with or apprehension about their health, or when they have an illness which modern medical science cannot cure. Alternative medicine is rarely alternative: it is almost always additional, at least when someone has a definable and serious illness.

Of course, it does not follow from the fact that epistemological relativism is incoherent and self-contradictory, and psychologically impossible to boot, that an entirely satisfactory account of human knowledge has been given by non-relativists.

THE SPREAD OF DOUBT

Now at one time arcane discussions about the nature, extent, and trustworthiness of human knowledge were confined to a small cadre of philosophers, who lived in ivory towers and either could not or did not want to make their arguments known to a wider public. It is not so long ago that only a very small percentage of the population attended university, and, of that small percentage, only a small percentage concerned itself with philosophy in general and epistemology in particular. However deadly earnest philosophers were in their work, philosophy amounted to a game, a pastime, or a hobby as far as the rest of society was concerned.

But there has been a vast increase in the number of people in the West who have undergone academic tertiary education, especially in the humanities. In Britain, for example, it is the government's wish that half of the population should attend university, and of course it is in the nature of modern bureaucracies that, by hook or by crook, they achieve the goals set for them by their political masters, even (or always) at the expense of the purpose behind those goals. In France, where passing the baccalaureat has always entitled a pupil to progress to higher education, the proportion of the population passing the baccalaureat has increased from 10 percent when my wife took it to 80 percent today. This might be an admirable sign of progress in education if, in the intervening period, that standard required to pass the baccalaureat had remained constant; but the evidence is pretty conclusive that the standard has fallen dramatically. It is true that changing conditions of life mean that children have to be taught different things from those they were once taught, which might make direct comparison difficult or complicated, but it is difficult to believe that any modern conditions have made basic literacy and numeracy less desirable or important than they once were.[33]

The fact remains that unprecedentedly large numbers of people, who would once have had little exposure to philosophical arguments, have now been exposed to epistemological relativism. It is probably true to say that, in proportion as their numbers increase, so their critical faculty decreases. They are therefore likely to accept on authority that there is no such thing as truth, that everything depends upon one's initial point of view, and that one opinion is as "valid" as another (the weasel-word "valid" has almost replaced the word "true"). They accept on authority that there is no authority: except, of course, what they themselves think, which is as good as what anyone else thinks. Intellectual weight is replaced by egotism.

This is not a good position from which to resist the claims of others in a principled way. Nagging uncertainty about one's own right to demand anything of others will be interspersed by gusts of hurt outrage that one's own rights are not being respected, but the latter will not last for long or lead to any long-term solution of any problem. Apathy masquerading as tolerance will alternate with short periods of violent reaction.

THE MULTICULTURALISM OF DAILY LIFE

Combined with philosophical relativism is the increasing practical relativism of everyday life, a vastly increased awareness that one's own way of doing things is not the only way of doing them. It is not only that the past is a foreign country where they do things differently; the present has become a foreign country where they do things differently.

---

33. A senior academic at Imperial College, one of Britain's most important institutions of scientific education, recently complained that British students wrote English less well than foreigners, whose second or even third language it was.

The cities in which most people in Europe live have changed out of all recognition in the last two or three decades. More than a third of the population of London was not born in Britain, let alone England;[34] the figure for Paris is a quarter. A few blocks from the center of Copenhagen, you would not know what country you are in. Once, when I drove into Antwerp, I thought I might as well have arrived in Morocco. Another time when I arrived at Manchester Airport, there was not a single European face in the throng in the arrivals hall. The figures for people of foreign origin are rising, though it is possible that a serious economic recession, depression, or slump might reverse the trend (though, if so, it will be the most active foreigners, not those dependent upon subventions from the state, who will be the first to leave).

I will return to the question of why it has become impermissible for anyone other than those of the worst kind, with the basest emotions, to express unease about this situation, indeed to say anything about it other than how exhilarating it is. For the moment, I will simply remark that the fact of human diversity has never been so inescapably present in the lives of people in Europe as now. People for whom sexual display is the principle meaning of life[35] live cheek-by-jowl with people for whom the uncovering of practically any flesh whatever is morally equivalent to prostitution. The variety of human customs, and moral justification of those customs, is made obvious as never before.

This self-evident variety is bound to have an effect on anyone who is minimally reflective. Nothing is the "natural," that is to say the unselfconscious, way to do anything anymore; everything becomes a matter of conscious choice. What would once have been accepted unquestioningly, because there seemed to be no alternative, is now open to contestation, for if other people do things

34. London has long been a magnet to outsiders, of course. It wasn't until the nineteenth century that London could maintain its population without inward migration. In the middle of the eighteenth century, a half of all children in London died before the age of five, yet it continued to grow. This suggests, incidentally, that life expectancy does not figure very highly in people's calculation of where to live.

35. A teacher told me of a seven year old who came crying to her that he had just been called a virgin. He did not know what it meant, but he knew it meant something horrible.

differently and yet survive, there can be no unanswerable reason for doing anything in any particular way. Contestation there has always been, of course; there have always been people who have deliberately challenged the *status quo*. But generally changes were wrought relatively slowly, not by the force of example before everyone's eyes, but by the imagining of a moral order that would be better than the existing one. And the aim of the contestation was generally a new uniformity in the way of living rather than a new variety in the way of living. Feminists, for example, did not want women merely to be able to work in the wider world than home and hearth; they wanted women actually to do so.[36]

CHOICE THE HIGHEST GOOD

Choice as a good in itself, even as the only good in itself, is now almost an unthinking orthodoxy in the West, and affects everything from economic policy to medical ethics. Life is conceived as a vast supermarket through which one moves with one's shopping trolley, fetching down ways of life from shelves marked "Existential choices." Today's choice does not affect or preclude tomorrow's choice; even Time's arrow is now believed to fly in more than one direction. Just as what you eat today does not determine what you eat tomorrow,[37] so what you are and what you do today does not determine what you are and what you do tomorrow.

This emphasis on choice as the measure of all things is mistaken, if only because nothing is the measure of *all* things. Patient

---

36. A proof of this is that the continuing relative dearth of women at the top of companies and other organizations is taken as evidence of the need for continued struggle against "patriarchy." It is not enough that formal legal barriers should have been removed; only absolute statistical equality will satisfy. For this to occur, however, women will either have to behave exactly as men, with the same tastes, the same ambitions, et cetera, or very drastic and in other respects counterproductive laws would have to be passed. What is demanded is not opportunity, but accomplished fact.

37. I suspect that culinary tropes are more important than is sometimes realized. Intellectuals, when they talk of multiculturalism as a doctrine rather than as a sociological phenomenon, are thinking of couscous today, chicken sagwalla tomorrow, cassoulet the day after, and sashimi the day after that.

autonomy has become the key concept of medical ethics, but many patients are only too willing and anxious to give themselves into the hands of others (and, of course, trust is a great ally of the doctor in overcoming illness, as mistrust is almost certainly an enemy). This desire to abandon choice may occur for a variety of reasons: some people may simply not be up to it intellectually, and rightfully want someone more expert than themselves to decide on their behalf in their best interests. Others may simply be too exhausted by illness to make the effort for themselves. (I was once in that situation, and I have no reason to regret having entrusted myself and my fate to the medical profession.)

At any rate, choice can give rise to anxiety and misery as well as to joy and happiness. The fable of Buridan's ass is instructive. Placed between two bales of equally tempting hay, the ass died of starvation because it could not make up its mind which bale to start eating. Besides, something that is unavoidable is often less intolerable than the same thing when it is believed to be avoidable. What makes the kind of marriages I have described above so appalling is that there is an alternative to them, or rather that there is an awareness of an alternative. Such marriages are far worse for daughters brought up in the West than for their mothers who had been brought up in a more traditional society. It is for this reason that totalitarian regimes are so anxious to prevent genuine information from elsewhere reaching their populations: such information transforms the unhappiness that seemed inevitable into the choice of the rulers and the consequence of what they do.

The view that every aspect of life is, should, or can be an endless choice between alternatives has at least two unfortunate psychological effects. First, it causes people to overestimate the degree to which they, or others, control events and conditions. It makes people unable to distinguish between what can and cannot be so controlled, so that they become unwilling to accept the fundamental existential limits of human existence, or the fact, obvious on reflection, that not all human desires are compatible, and that therefore dissatisfaction is a permanent guest at life's feast (you cannot be safe and adventurous at the same time, as investors in Mr. Madoff's scheme found to their cost). When the world proves refractory to one's desires, as it always does to some extent, the overestimation of the powers of men to mold the world according to their will leads to a state of resentment, because one's dissatisfaction must be *someone's* fault. And resentment is one of the worst states of mind, for it is like fatalism, except that it is without acceptance of the fate.

The second baleful effect of the view of life as an existential supermarket is that no choice is taken very seriously, because a whole future of choices spreads endlessly before one, like a landscape without a horizon. The freedom demanded by this view of life is absolute, without constraint at all: no choice should foreclose on any other future choice, and vistas should remain forever open. It is as if people went on a journey and, coming to a fork in the road, turned left because the landscape was believed to be more interesting along it, while simultaneously demanding that they reach the destination attainable only by turning right. The reluctance of men to "commit" to a woman is a complaint often heard in recent years, and (if the figures of young adults living in single-person households are to be believed) is a real phenomenon.[38]

The nature of freedom is here mistaken. It is obvious that for human beings to be free, they need to live in a rule-bound society. There is an analogy here with language. There are many modern educationists who believe that teaching children the standard grammar of their language, which they may not learn at home or in their social environment, is harmful, not only to their self-esteem because it suggests to them that something that they are already doing, naturally as it were, is not perfect, but to their creativity. In other words, such teaching limits their freedom by putting them in a linguistic straitjacket. It is obvious, however, that mastery of the standard language (whether or not they choose to exercise it)

---

38. I once had a patient whose long-term girlfriend attempted suicide because he repeatedly refused to ask her to marry him. He couldn't understand it, he said; after all, marriage was only a piece of paper. "If it's only a piece of paper," I asked him, "why don't you sign it?" The failure to commit reminds me of some literary parties that I have attended, at which my interlocutor has surveyed the people in the room while talking to me, on the lookout for someone more famous, more important, or more useful to his career or as a contact than myself to talk to (fortunately for him, always present, and often in large numbers).

widens the scope of their freedom very considerably, and makes available to them far more than it precludes, though it remains true that there is no gain without loss. It surely depends upon which the person considers to be greater or more important.

ALL OPTIONS OPEN

The person who wants to keep all his options open does not accept that every gain entails a loss, that turning left precludes arriving at a destination only to be reached by turning right. This lack of acceptance is no doubt the result of a loss of religious sensibility, with its insistence that "my kingdom is not of this world," that man, by virtue of Original Sin, his biological nature, or whatever you want to call it, is incapable of achieving a state of perfect (and therefore permanent) happiness. This is precisely what the person who wants to foreclose on no possibility cannot accept: he is a utopian, not for society as a whole, but for himself.

He therefore finds what he thinks are good reasons to reject such ideas as commitment to another person to the exclusion of others. Such commitment, he is the first to point out, leads as often as not to hypocrisy. This is certainly true. The briefest survey of literature would be sufficient to demonstrate that infidelity is an important and recurrent theme of poems, plays, novels, and short stories. The study of DNA shows that about a tenth of children are not fathered by the person who is generally thought to be their father. As for the Pauline notion that he who so much as looks at a woman who is not his wife has committed adultery in his heart, it is so unrealistic that it can be dismissed out of hand.

Only a moment's reflection is necessary, however, to realize the insufficiency of all this to draw any large conclusion, such as that marriage is a worthless institution that ought to be abolished even as an option.[39] What can be said of infidelity can be

---

39. The headline of a recent story in the liberal (and best) British newspaper *The Guardian* read, "Marriage is legalized prostitution." In other contexts (i.e. of prostitution) prostitutes are, of course, called "sex-workers." In other words, sex is legitimate only if it occurs out of wedlock.

said of robbery or murder: however much they are condemned, and however draconian the laws against them, they continue to be committed, and will always continue to be committed. No one, as far as I am aware, has ever denied the necessity of a prohibition against killing on the grounds that it cannot work, and that murderers there will always be: where human beings are concerned, nothing ever works, at least not in the sense that it produces precisely and only the result desired.

The effect and purpose of relativism, both that which is based upon philosophical abstractions such as the impossibility of founding human knowledge upon the rock of indubitable principles, and that which is based upon the anthropological fact of human variety, is to dissolve inherited boundaries that place restraints upon personal conduct, restraints which are unwanted because they are thought to be not a precondition of human freedom (as, of course, some restraints are), but inherently an attack on the liberty of the individual.

The obituary of a writer that appeared in Le Monde in 2008 gave an extraordinary example of this desire to dissolve boundaries in the name of personal freedom. The writer in question was a true *soixante-huitard*, who took seriously the slogan that it is forbidden to forbid. He was the author of several books in the 1970s that had had some success at the time, but which have since fallen into oblivion. He died alone in an isolated cottage in the country, where his body was not found for a month, so socially isolated had he become. The obituary printed the kernel of his thought in large bold letters: that sexual relations and the state should have nothing whatever to do with one another.

Nothing? Can he really have meant *nothing?* That the law should not place any boundaries whatever on sexual activity, however defined? This was not an appeal to shift boundaries, which is sometimes reasonable; it was a call for their abolition altogether. There should be no limits according to age, place, or type of activity. If there is no law, everything is permitted.

Of course, one isolated intellectual does not make a social trend, and by comparison with Britain, France remains a well-ordered society, if one that remains liable from time to time to outbreaks of social unrest. Underlying the thin crust of good order bubbles a magma of adolescent longing, waiting its occasion to burst through yet again. Every ten years in France, the latest in 2008, there is an outpouring of nostalgia for the events of 1968, when to be young was very heaven, when to hurl a cobblestone at a policeman or a shop window, when to overturn a car and alarm the adults seemed like a noble thing to do (and not to do it correspondingly ignoble). The famous and fatuous slogan "It is forbidden to forbid" has by no means been forgotten; and the freest society is supposedly the one in which there are the fewest prohibitions. And this applies as much to the informal prohibitions of social pressure as to those of law. The claims of the individual are paramount as never before. As the French supermarket chain Champion claims, *le client est roi*, the customer is king, and what is life (as life in our cities now amply demonstrates) but an existential supermarket? I am reminded of the description of the poet Shelley's character in Walter Bagehot's *Estimations in Criticism*:

> The love of liberty is peculiarly natural to the simple impulsive mind [such as his]. It feels irritated at the idea of a law; it fancies it does not need it . . . . Government seems absurd—an incubus. It has hardly patience to estimate particular institutions; it wants to begin again—to make a *tabula rasa* of all which men have created or devised; for they seem to have been created on a false system, for an object it does not understand.

The question is why a character that seemed exceptional in Shelley's time should have become almost the norm among thinking men, and the followers of thinking men?

6.

WHY ARE WE LIKE THIS (I)?

The idea that it is forbidden to forbid is a peculiar and even absurd one, that could not have gained wide currency for most of human history. It is no more conformable to common sense than the opposite gloomy view, that men are so insufficient and unsuited to freedom that their every last act should be laid down by authority, political or religious, and that what is not forbidden should be required, and *vice versa*.

Of course, even when men feel completely free to behave as they choose, they usually end up behaving, if not like everybody else exactly, at least like a lot of other people. There is safety in numbers, and the desire for safety is not easily abolished; and in any case there are not so many different ways of behaving present in most people's imagination. The injunction or command to be yourself (as if you could be anyone else) ends up being the same as the command to be exactly as your neighbor. Thus the slogan that "it is forbidden to forbid" does not result in the abolition of rules as such, but in their replacement by different rules.

A HERD OF INDIVIDUALS

Thus comes about a state of mind (or soul, if you prefer) that is characteristic of our era, and is a mass phenomenon to be seen everywhere on our streets: individualism without individuality. People who are unwilling to brook the slightest restriction imposed by any authority are completely subservient to the tastes, opinions, and mores of their peers, and intolerant of deviation from them by others. Egotism goes hand in hand with uniformity: a rather odd alliance when you think of it.

Such uniformity is not by any means new. A photograph of a human crowd now shows no more uniformity than a photograph of a crowd of fifty or a hundred years ago. What is new is that the uniform feel a need to be different:[40] to claim to be unique, to have an explicit right to be and to express their uniqueness, and to have it recognized by others. The appreciation of the need for a subtle interplay between obedience to authority and convention on the one hand, and personal liberty on the other, has been lost,

---

40. Nothing could be more alien from the modern sensibility than the thought expressed at the end of Antonio Machado's poem *He andado muchos caminos:*

> *Son buenas gentes que viven,*
> *laboran, pasan y suenan,*
> *y un dia como tantos*
> *descansan bajo la tierra.*

> They are good people who live,
> work, walk and dream,
> And one day like so many others
> Lie down to rest under the earth.

It is surely the case that humility and lack of self-importance are a large component of the goodness of the good people to whom Machado here refers. Compare this verse with a verse of Sylvia Plath's that breathes self-obsession and self-importance:

> Dying is an art,
> Like everything else.
> I do it exceptionally well.
> I do it so it feels like hell.
> I do it so it feels real.
> I guess you could say I have a call.

even among reflective intellectuals. That liberty needs a constitution in which to flourish—an informal social one as much as a formal political one—is scarcely appreciated. It is not a coincidence that one of the three French national newspapers should be called *Libération*, without there being the slightest indication of what it is that the readers are supposed to be liberated from. One suspects that it is from the frustrations of life, as if a life could be lived without the frustration that inevitably arises from the incompatible desires that reside in every human breast. There is a longing to be freed from the tyranny of the existential limitations of human existence.

No doubt the decline of religion accounts for the rise in self-obsession and self-importance that is everywhere observable. One of the great advantages of the Christian philosophy was that it managed to reconcile the unique importance of each man with humility. Every man was important in the eyes of God, and in that sense was at home in the universe because the universe was expressly created for beings such as he. His every action was known to God, and was therefore not without significance, however ordinary in other respects it might be; moreover, death itself was not without meaning, nor was it the end of his existence. Yet, by comparison with the author of his being, he was infinitely small, as indeed was every other human being. However scholarly a man might be, God, being omniscient, was infinitely more knowledgeable; howsoever powerful a man might believe himself, it was finally God who disposed, so that all human power was both illusory and transitory. In the midst of life we are in death, the funeral service of the Church of England puts it; and it might have added, in the midst of importance we are in insignificance.

I am not here concerned with whether this outlook is philosophically justified: with whether God exists, and if He does, with whether he is more interested in our doings and more solicitous of our welfare than He is with those of an ant, for example. All I am concerned to point out is that the religious outlook referred to above manages the difficult feat of assuring man of his supreme importance without giving him a swollen head.

SECULARIZATION

The secularization of Europe is hardly any secret. Religion's long, melancholy, withdrawing roar, as Matthew Arnold put it, is a roar no longer, and hardly even a murmur. In France, the oldest and most important daughter of the Church, fewer than 5 percent of the population attend Mass regularly. The English national church has long been an object of amusement and derision among the intelligent and educated, and the current Archbishop of Canterbury succeeds in uniting the substance and appearance of utter foolishness, and unworldliness not with sanctity, but with sanctimony. In Wales, where non-conformist Christianity was the dominant moral and cultural influence, most of the chapels found everywhere have been converted into private residences by architects and interior decorators. A Welshman is now much more likely to be found in a supermarket on a Sunday morning than in a chapel; the vast outpourings of pietistic writings, both in English and Welsh, now molder into disintegration on the shelves of second-hand booksellers, who themselves are closing down daily. In the Netherlands, some elements of the religious *pillarisation* of the state remain: for example, state-funded television channels are still allotted to the Protestants and Catholics respectively. But while the shell of religious *pillarisation* still exists, the substance has gone: watching the channels, you would not easily be able to guess which was Catholic and which was Protestant.

Perhaps it is Ireland that offers the most startling example of secularization in Europe because it was a late starter. Late starters, however, are often very apt pupils; they catch up fast, and even surpass their mentors. Not long ago, Catholicism was essential to the identity of the country, not surprisingly in view of its long domination by a Protestant minority. When I first went to Ireland, the priest was a god among men, people stood aside to let him pass; everyone wanted at least one priest in the family, and a bishop was like a local satrap. No respectable family did not count a nun among its members. As for the Archbishop of Dublin, his word was law; the politicians might propose, but he it was who disposed. He had the virtual veto power on any legislation.

In the historical bat of an eyelid, all that has gone, beyond any hope (or fear) of restoration. It would hardly be too much to say that the Church is now reviled in Ireland, at least by that class of person who ultimately sets the tone of society, namely the metropolitan intelligentsia. I suspect that if you now performed a word-association test in Ireland using the word "priest," it would more often than not evoke the response of "paedophile," "child-abuser," or (at best) "hypocrite."

No doubt the church had itself in part to blame for this revulsion against it. Ireland had indeed been oppressively priest-ridden since its independence and the church had shown itself all too interested in temporal power, imposing its views about everything on the state. A church too closely identified with any particular political regime or social and economic order is asking for trouble when (as eventually it always will) the regime or order changes, as it did in Ireland at the end of the 1980s. Economic nationalism and attempted autarchy gave way to openness to the world, with huge economic success, and the church stood accused of having impeded Ireland's progress by its obscurantism for eighty years. Just as importantly, scandals of the sexual abuse of children by priests saw the light of day, which the church attempted to cover up, minimize, or deny. These scandals and the dishonest way in which the church responded to them were eagerly seized upon by the anti-clerical party; but I suspect that animus towards the church pre-dated the scandals, which were merely a pretext to attack a previously invulnerable institution. I think it unlikely that in a society such as the Irish, knowledge of the behavior of a few priests came altogether as a surprise, as something new and completely unsuspected.

Be that as it may, priests were eagerly tarred with the same brush so that many of them, in Dublin at least, became reluctant to walk out in public in priestly garb.[41] Until I met priests in

---

41. In Mexico, since the revolution, priests have been prohibited by law from appearing anywhere except in church in such garb. But Ireland is surely the first country in modern peacetime western Europe where priests are actually afraid to proclaim their vocation.

Dublin walking in mufti, I had never met any who did not wear clerical garb for everyday use; and (what is surely one of the most remarkable reversals in recent history) a Roman Catholic priest probably feels more at his ease, less likely to meet with hostility or disrespect, in England than in Ireland.

The secularization of Ireland is but an instance of the secularization, much longer in its development, of the whole of western Europe. The extremely low birth-rates in Spain and Italy, the lowest ever recorded in any modern society, suggest that the populations of these traditionally Catholic countries do not pay much practical attention to the teachings of their church. Throughout the Catholic lands congregations dwindle and vocations are few, much below replacement level, and priests must now be imported from the Third World. Recently in Belgium I saw an old and venerable convent where the few remaining nuns were all in their eighties and would never be replaced. When they died, their convent, presumably, would be turned into luxury apartments for unwed professional couples with no children.

Thus the religious approach to life that I described above is as alien to modern Europeans as that of Zoroastrianism or Zen Buddhism: it is no part of their mental world. A contrast is often drawn between Europe and America in this respect, Americans having supposedly retained a much more religious outlook on life than Europeans. I think, however, this distinction is much less than is sometimes claimed, so much of American religion having very little about it that suggests true or abiding belief rather than social conformity. In their attitudes to health, illness, and death, for example, they are not much different from Europeans; nor are they much different from how they would be if they professed no belief in God.

For good or ill, God is dead in Europe and I do not see much chance of revival except in the wake of catastrophe. Not quite everything has been lost of the religious attitude, however; individuals still think of themselves as a being of unique importance, but without the countervailing humility of considering themselves to have a duty towards the author of their being, a being inconceivably larger than themselves. Far from inducing a more modest self-conception in man, the loss of religious belief has inflamed his self-importance enormously.

LIFE WITHOUT TRANSCENDENCE

For the person with no transcendent religious belief (and that now means the overwhelming majority of Europeans), this life is all he has. He must therefore preserve and prolong it at all costs— and not only preserve it and prolong it, but live it to the full. Death for him is extinction, the void, eternal nothingness; and however much philosophers seek to persuade us that it is illogical more to fear an infinite oblivion after our death than to regret the infinite oblivion before our birth, the fact is that most men still fear not merely the process of death (which philosophers concede is not entirely irrational), but also the nothingness of death itself. For most people—I won't say quite all, David Hume perhaps being an exception[42]—the fact of having once lived makes a big difference between the pre-birth oblivion and the post-death one.

But what is living to the full—or to the max, as young people now put it? There are not many Hamlets about who could be enclosed in a nutshell and count themselves kings of infinite space. For most people, living to the full means consuming as much as possible, having as many experiences as possible, and not only many experiences, but the most extreme experiences possible. The infinitudes of learning and scholarship, which can give to a life a purpose without end, to the very last day of a man's earthly existence,[43] are not and cannot be suited to the great majority of mankind. This is not to despise or denigrate the great majority of mankind: not only would a population composed entirely of scholars soon starve to death, but it would not even be very pleasant while it lasted. Scholars are necessary, but by no means sufficient.

---

42. Though Doctor Johnson did not think so.

43. J. K. Galbraith published his last book at the age of ninety-six; Nirad C. Chaudhuri at the age of a hundred.

The problem with consumption is that it soon ceases to satisfy. How else can one explain the crowds that assemble in every city center in Europe (and increasingly elsewhere) every weekend to buy what they cannot possibly need and perhaps do not even want? Will yet another shirt or pair of shoes supply a need for a transcendent purpose? At best there will be a brief moment of elation, followed soon after by prolonged indifference to whatever it is that has been bought. The length of the moment of elation will be proportional to scarcity, for in most cases (again, not quite all perhaps) appreciation and enjoyment of new material possessions is in proportion to scarcity.

The same might be said of the experiences that people seek, the experiences that they feel they must seek if they are to live life to the full. Sports become more extreme in their competitive urgency, holidays ever more exotic, films more violent, broadcasting more vulgar, the expression of emotion more crude and obvious (compare advertisements showing people enjoying themselves sixty years ago and now). Mouths are open and screams, either of joy or pain, emerge. Quiet satisfaction is no satisfaction at all; what is not expressed grossly is not deemed to have been expressed.

Of course, there might be transcendent purposes or meanings to life apart from that provided by religion. I have already mentioned scholarship, by which I mean also scientific research as well as the sifting of written evidence and philosophical reflection more typical of the humanities; but a life of scholarship can never be that of more than a small minority of the population.

A transcendent meaning to life can be sought in politics of a certain kind. Marxism might have been deficient as an explanation of the world; its prophecies might have been refuted, as far as undated prophecies can ever be refuted; and as a guide to the establishment of regimes in practice, its record has been uniformly atrocious, leading to more complete tyrannies than any previously experienced by mankind, that has hardly been lacking in imagination in this matter. But one thing it did do for millions of people, at least for a time: it gave them the feeling that their lives were a contribution to the immanent meaning of history, and that they were a contribution to the denouement of history, when all contradictions would be resolved, all desires fulfilled, and all human relations easy, spontaneous, friendly, and loving. It was obvious nonsense, of course, but not more obvious nonsense than the religious ideas of those whose religious ideas we do not happen to share.

So long as the Soviet Union existed, Marxism gathered unto itself, in its various forms, most of those who sought transcendence in politics. The search for transcendence in politics did not cease, however, with the transformation of the Soviet Union from an ideological state to a secret-police mafia state. Marxism was discredited apart from a few academics and aging faithful;[44] the impulse and allegiance transferred seamlessly to other causes.

A NEW PAGAN TRANSCENDENCE

Chief among these was the environment. The threatened cataclysm was not to be brought about any longer by the unbearable contradictions of capitalism, but by the unsustainable destruction of the environment brought about by human activity. As with the final crisis of capitalism, however, nothing but a complete transformation would do; and the more extreme the allegedly necessary changes, the more extremists could pass them off as prescriptions for change; extremists could pose as the saviors of the human race. Just as Leninists knew what was good for the proletariat, thereby conferring on themselves a gratifyingly providential role, so the environmentalists now know what is good for humanity and likewise confer on themselves a providential role. The beauty of preservation of the environment as a cause is that it is so large that it would justify almost any ends used to achieve it, for a livable environment is the *sine qua non* of everything else. You can

---

44. In 1988, I think it was, I stood in a line to gain entry to Lenin's mausoleum. Behind me was an American in his sixties who, to judge from his accent, was from Brooklyn.

"This country is the hope of the world," he said to me.
"What?" I replied. "And you still can't buy any potatoes."

demonstrate and riot for the good of humanity to your heart's content; your questions about what life is for are answered.

THE TRANSCENDENCE OF SMALL CAUSES

Some people are able to find transcendence in lesser, but still large, causes: such as nationalism, animal rights, or feminism. The unity of the United Kingdom, for example, has now been threatened by a resurgent Scottish nationalism. This was in large part a superficial phenomenon, having been stimulated by the release of a Hollywood film, *Braveheart*.[45] When the world financial crisis broke, however, in the course of which both large Scottish banks collapsed and had to be rescued by the British government, support for Scottish independence, at least north of the border, declined somewhat (there is now the rather peculiar situation that a larger proportion of the English population favor Scottish independence than of the Scottish population). The reasons for this are not difficult to understand. Scotland receives large subsidies from England, such that (according to an article in *The Spectator*) only fifteen thousand Scotsmen are net contributors to the treasury, while all the rest, that is to say five million, receive more than they pay. In these circumstances, independence and the loss of English subsidies would entail very considerable social and economic upheaval, not lightly to be undertaken in times that, at best, are

---

45. The extent to which young people's knowledge of history and the world is shaped by film is remarkable, as is their unawareness of its insufficiency as a source of knowledge. Not long ago I met a seventeen-year-old girl in England who was studying history at "advanced" level in school. I asked her what aspect of history she was then studying. "The Rwandan genocide," she replied, with an expression approaching that of moral self-satisfaction. Having myself visited Rwanda, this was a subject that interested me (I leave aside the question as to whether teaching so contemporary an event is the best way to instill a sense of history in the young), and I asked what her source material was, what books she was reading, etc. The only source she was able to name was the film *Hotel Rwanda*, which she had been enjoined to watch. She was blithely unaware of the insufficiency of this as an historical document, as she was unaware that the Belgians had once ruled in Rwanda, and that to the south there was a country called Burundi where events had tended to be a mirror image of those in Rwanda. Everything is evidence of something, of course, but a Hollywood film is hardly evidence of what happened in history. She was undergoing an education not of the mind, but of the emotions—and cheap emotions at that.

those of economic retraction. By contrast, Scottish independence might decrease the tax burden on the English—though I suspect it would not, for governments rarely give up moneys that they raise, and can easily find new things upon which to waste them.

Nevertheless, there are some genuine, strong, and deep nationalists, deeply attached to the cause, which no doubt gives transcendent purpose to their life. A nation, after all, is more than the sum of people now living in its geographical area or within a particular jurisdiction: a nationalist communes with the past and with the future, and in that sense fulfills the contract that Burke says that we have, or ought to have, not only with the present and future but also with the past: for if we disdain to notice, appreciate, or preserve what our ancestors have left us, what we have inherited, what reason have we for supposing that future generations will be any kinder to us and our efforts, to what they inherit from us? That is why a sense of the past (which the nationalist always has, however distorted or given to special pleading his historiography may be) is so important in giving man that feeling of transcendence necessary if he is to avoid the opposite, a nihilistic despair that life is just one damn thing after another, and that no event has any meaning or significance beyond its arbitrary occurrence.[46]

The fact that nationalism of the Scottish type is often in the material interest of a small class of political entrepreneurs does not alter the fact that it answers a man's need for the transcendent in his life. If Scotland were to become genuinely independent, at least as independent as membership of the European Union now allows any member state to be, it would require (for example) the establishment of an entire diplomatic service, with ambassadors, first secretaries, etc., and a large supportive bureaucracy.[47] Thanks to the expansion of tertiary education, there is a large fund of highly educated people neither fitted for commerce nor trained to a profession (or, if they have been trained to a profession, find it

---

46. I shall deal later with the disastrous consequences of the cult of the present moment on European architecture.

47. It goes without saying that the English diplomatic service and bureaucracy would not be correspondingly reduced in size.

too crowded to satisfy their longing for easy distinction). What a splendid opportunity a whole new diplomatic corps would be for these people, to say nothing of all the other posts that would have to be created in the new state! Nor should we forget the increased opportunities for good old-fashioned graft: when Mr. Blair, with the kind of self-righteous impulsivity that characterized him, decided to devolve powers on to a newly created Scottish parliament (which led to the peculiar and anomalous situation that Scottish members elected to the Westminster parliament could vote on purely English matters but not on Scottish ones), the new parliament building in Edinburgh, which was originally estimated to cost £40 million, cost £400 million to construct, enough, one would imagine, not only to have made quite a number of people very rich, but to convert certain kinds of businessmen to the benefits of yet further devolution and independence.

As I have mentioned, none of this alters the ability of nationalism to answer a man's need for the transcendent. Even if the nationalist should be deceived, that is to say self-deceived, as to the true motives of his nationalism (if the true motives of anyone about anything could be known beyond peradventure), the important thing, from the point of view of the successful achievement of transcendence, is that he should be so deceived.

But of course nationalism since the end of the Second World War has not been a respectable source of personal transcendence in Europe, except at the periphery, among the smaller nations, and understandably so. I shall deal with the burdens of history at some length later on; suffice it for now to say that no one could contemplate the history of Romanian nationalism in the twentieth century, say, and wish for its return, whatever the sense of personal transcendence it gave to those who embraced it.[48] One

---

48. It is a commonplace of history that, where oppression of national minorities is concerned, especially in central and eastern Europe, the lines of Jonathan Swift are highly suggestive:

So nat'ralists observe, a flea
Hath smaller fleas that on him prey,

of the first things the Baltic states did after independence from the Soviet Union was to make life difficult for the many Russians living in them, no doubt understandably so in view of recent history; and no doubt also the disproportion of power between those states and Russia saved the Russians from still worse treatment. The liberation, autonomy, and independence, so-called, of Kosovo were followed immediately by the ethnic cleansing of Serbs and gypsies. History has an unpleasant habit of revenging itself upon the innocent, or at least those who are guilty to only a very minor extent.[49]

In the new Europe, in any case, nationalism is something of an anomaly, given that the drive is to the elimination of national boundaries and national sovereignty. It may yet prove that the bloody break-up of Yugoslavia was much ado about nothing, or nothing very much; for having broken away from the federation and achieved national sovereignty at such great cost, the successor states have lost little time in handing over their sovereign powers to a much larger federation, which is much less likely to be responsive to their particular needs and concerns than the federation from which they had just broken away. The Basque terrorist group ETA may thus be said to be bombing its way not to national independence, but (whether it knows or acknowledges it or not) to well-paid, feather-bedded bureaucratic positions in Brussels, with generous expenses and free fine dining. The same can be said of the Corsican separatists, though it seems to me

And these have smaller fleas that bite 'em,
And so proceed *ad infinitum.*

If only President Wilson had kept these lines in mind.

49. When the British publisher Victor Gollancz visited Germany shortly after the end of the Second World War to investigate and report on the appalling conditions in which the Germans were when living, many people would say to him that the Germans deserved everything they got. Gollancz, who was Jewish and whose publishing firm had spent the 1930s publishing books warning of the Nazi peril, could not be accused of the slightest of Nazi sympathies, replied to his vengeful interlocutors with devastating simplicity: "And the children?"

unlikely that they will ever achieve even those somewhat prosaic, though lucrative, goals.

ANTI-NATIONALIST TRANSCENDENCE

The European project, as it is sometimes called, is of course the very opposite of nationalism: it is anti-nationalism, or at least anti-small-scale or petty nationalism. (One might plausibly construe it as an attempt to build one large, world-bestriding European nation, that is to say a form of megalomania.) But is the European project the kind of political ideal that can give transcendence to anyone but a half-mad visionary? Does the European Union cause the heart of anyone other than a bureaucrat in search of a comfortable billet to miss a beat?

The question is not quite as easy to answer as might at first sight appear, the temptation being to answer it with the kind of guffaw with which one greets a patently ridiculous suggestion. For the fact is that, historically, national and other identities have been forged deliberately where they did not exist before, and an absence of feeling turned into a very real, or at least a very strong, feeling. We are so accustomed, when we think politically, to assume the necessity for and immutability of nation states that we are a little like those people who assumed the immutability of species before the publication of *The Origin of Species*.

A few examples will suffice. Even the oldest-established European states such as France had difficulty in establishing a national language, accepted and used everywhere on the national territory, as late as the nineteenth century.[50] Italy—Metternich's famous geographical expression—is another case in point, Tuscan Italian being imposed rather than adopted spontaneously as the national language (though it had long been the *lingua franca* of the polite

---

50. A Welsh friend of mine, slightly younger than I, told me that as a child she had been punished at school for speaking Welsh in the playground—though there was not the slightest chance that she would fail to learn English properly. In fact, she had already mastered it.

and educated of the peninsula). National feeling had to be stirred in Eastern Europe, it didn't just emerge spontaneously. I doubt that any Wallachian of the seventeenth century would have replied, "I am a Romanian" to the question, "Who and what are you?"

Turkey is an important case also. Of course the expression "Turk" existed before Turkey came (or, rather, was brought) into being, but it was not straightforwardly one of national rather than cultural description. No one, I think, can doubt the strength of Turkish national feeling, and yet there is clearly something fragile about it too, as if Turkishness were a lesson only recently learnt and imperfectly mastered, and therefore likely to be forgotten. It is still an offense in Turkey to insult or bring into disrepute the founder of modern Turkey, Mustafa Kemal, and not long ago I met a professor in Turkey who had been imprisoned briefly for having done precisely that, though his criticism of Ataturk was measured and couched in academic terms, suggesting that his policies had not always been better than those of the Ottoman sultans. American nationality, for example, is clearly more securely grounded or entrenched than Turkish, because you can say what you like there about George Washington and all the Founding Fathers without fear of retribution: for example, that they were slave-owning hypocrites motivated by the fear that Lord Mansfield's famous judgment that a slave was free once his feet touched British soil might soon be extended to the colonies. It was an American professor who proposed this thesis, and suffered no worse consequences for having done so than a book that was remaindered.

Turkish nationalism was a deliberate and conscious response to the decline of the Ottoman Empire, which itself was made evident, if not brought about, by the rise of nationalism in its European territories. If the Ottomans could not beat them, it had to join them, and the Turks were, after all, the core of their population. Turkish national feeling, including that of xenophobia, did not develop overnight, however: as late as 1922, there were 2,000,000 Greeks still living in Turkey, and their descendents would probably be there still had the Greek government not so foolishly decided (with British and French encouragement) to try to re-create a Greek empire in Asia Minor by taking advantage of supposed Turkish weakness after the end of the First World War, and invading.

The Armenian genocide, which Turkey has so generally, repeatedly, and vigorously denied, extenuated, or minimized, was more the product of Turkish nationalism than of Ottomanism (if that ramshackle empire can be said to have had anything resembling an -ism). In so far as there was any provocation at all, it came from Armenian nationalism, the Armenians having been the Ottoman's "Loyal Nation" until the 1870s. (I do not mean to imply that there can ever be a justification for the cold-hearted massacre of entire populations.) The Armenian genocide—or massacres, as Turks prefer to call the episode, on the unconvincing grounds that no specific orders to carry out a genocide have ever been found—is so sensitive a subject in Turkey because it is so intimately bound up with the founding of the Republic which is the object of a fragile secular cult, now open to challenge from the Islamists, which is religious in all but its lack of a divinity, unless you count Ataturk as a divinity, with his mausoleum-shrine in Ankara, his monopoly on bank-notes, his bust in every town square and his picture in every business establishment, and the laws to protect him from blasphemy. It is difficult to imagine Clovis being treated the same way in France, or even Rurik in Russia; but, as we shall see, Turkey's problems with its history are by no means unique to it.

Further afield, we can see how nations that did not previously exist can come into existence, whose citizens learn to feel some emotional attachment to a new political entity.

It is one of the heads of accusation against European colonialism in Africa that it drew artificial boundaries, often with a ruler, on the map of the continent, without regard to geographical or (more importantly) human realities. I think this is a false accusation, except in so far as I think that the European countries had no business in the first place to be dividing Africa up between themselves.

These boundaries were inherited by the newly independent African states, and, in one of the few wise political decisions that have emerged from the continent ever since, the Organization of

African Unity decided that those boundaries should be inviolate, however indefensible they might be in the abstract. The Organization clearly saw what is obvious (if only the obvious were always so clearly seen!): that attempted revisions of boundaries on the basis of ethnic or geographical realities would lead to endless war.

The problem with the artificial boundaries, however, was that they created political entities to which no one felt their primary political allegiance. This is not to say that better boundaries could, even with the best will in the world (which is always lacking in human affairs), have been drawn, because the social and political realities of Africa made it peculiarly unsuited to the creation of a system of nation states. Once the European states had divided up the continent in the way they did, however, the creation of nation states was virtually inevitable; there was no going back to the pre-colonial polities that the Europeans had destroyed, even where they chose indirect rule as their mode of domination.

A NEW IDENTITY

The new nation states were fragile, of course, perhaps (but not entirely) because most of them contained many ethnicities aggregated pell-mell into one new nation.[51] This said, it is clear that some kind of national feeling and character are emerging in the various states in Africa because—the boundaries having been held inviolate for some considerable time, all the longer because such a proportion of the population is young and has known no other political reality—the people within those boundaries really do now share some historical experience, good, bad, or atrocious as it might be. The vast majority of Nigerians, for example, has known nothing but independent Nigeria; and while they remain

---

51. Interestingly, some of those African states that did more or less conform to political, ethnic, and geographical realities—Rwanda, Burundi, and Somalia—did not do better than those that did not. Botswana, on the other hand, another of the states than conformed more or less to those realities, was a great success story, one of the very few in post-independence Africa. Swaziland was a relative success, while Losotho was an ordinary failure. There seems to be no hard and fast rule about this matter.

divided into some three hundred or so ethnicities (depending on what counts as an ethnicity), the fact is that they do now have something, their Nigerianness if you like, in common. For one thing, Nigeria is surrounded by countries that have a different *lingua franca* from its own: French instead of English. That in itself gives it a distinguishing feature; and geographical distance alone would give Nigerians a different identity from other African Anglophones, even if there were nothing else to distinguish them (which is far from being the case, since modern Nigerian history is *sui generis*).

With the passage of time, a political entity that at its inception corresponded to no feelings of belonging among the people under its jurisdiction comes gradually to claim some portion of that population's affective loyalty or (what is not the same thing) personal identity. People come to feel and define themselves as Nigerian, not only to describe themselves to others, but to themselves. It is not only that people who belong in other respects to antagonistic groups cheer for the same side in sporting contests against other countries, feeling exhilaration, however fleeting, on victory and despondency, however equally fleeting, on defeat, but they actually come to share some characteristics that might reasonably be termed national.

More than twenty years ago, a Nigerian journalist, Peter Enahoro, published an amusing little book titled *How to Be a Nigerian*. He suggested that the national characteristics, recognized but not viewed wholly favorably by neighbors, were brashness, a tendency to boast, loudness, sociability, energy, an elastic approach to financial probity, and a sense of humor. (This is certainly true: no people known to me are more able to laugh at themselves than Nigerians, though many have as well what is not an opposite quality, an ability to reflect seriously.) Certainly, few people in West Africa have any difficulty in recognizing a Nigerian as such when they meet one, and I am able to distinguish Nigerians without difficulty from, say, Ghanaians, another Anglophone West African people of a country cobbled together by colonial boundary-makers.

This brief excursus has revealed several important points: that national identities are often not given as in nature, but socially and ideologically constructed, sometimes successfully; that federations of nations tend to fall apart, often in terrible bloodshed; but that what replaces them is quite often no better; and that the seeming alternative to federation, namely absolute national sovereignty, is often hostage to a vile, hate-mongering nationalism.

7.

WHY ARE WE LIKE THIS (II)?

There is nothing absurd, then, in the abstract about an attempt to create a pan-European identity. Other identities, no less likely at the outset, have been forged. And indeed there is a glimmering of a European identity already, in the sense that (for example) Europeans in America tend to feel distinct from Americans not only in a national, but a continental sense. Brought up on an off-shore island whose inhabitants think that, when there is fog in the Channel, the Continent is isolated, I nevertheless feel greatly more *chez moi* in France, Germany, Italy, or Spain than I do when I visit the United States, and this despite barriers of language.

EVERYBODY A COMMUNITY OF IDENTITIES

Personal identities, and loyalties to groups and institutions, are layered. A person who felt himself to be defined by a single characteristic would be a monomaniac, and not the kind of person we should like to spend much time with. Attempts have been made for political purposes to instill monomaniacal personal identities into whole populations, that trump all other aspects of their identity (the quality of being a German, for example, or a proletarian), so that all practical and moral questions are to be decided in the light of that identity, but these attempts have had effects to which I do not need to draw attention. Islamic fundamentalism is the latest attempt to forge a seamless, unlayered, and unidimensional identity, according to which a good Muslim is perfectly in unison with other good Muslims, because his every thought is the same as theirs, and perfectly opposed to everyone who is not a good Muslim. A man's identity being necessarily and unavoidably plural, such that in one situation he thinks of himself as principally an x, and in another as principally a y, the scheme of providing him with an unlayered identity, such that in all possible situations he thinks of himself as a z and nothing but a z, is bound to fail, as a moment's reflection would confirm. Unfortunately, the sheer impossibility of a political goal has never deterred a fanatic of the cause from pursuing it, and little does more harm than the pursuit of the impossible, at least when it is aimed at without a sense of irony.[52]

No man, then, has a national identity and no other. It is obvious that a national identity can trump other aspects of a man's identity in certain situations: a total war, for example. So can other aspects of his identity, in other situations. But any supposedly perfect union with others is bound to fracture once the situation that brought that union into being has passed. Milton, in *The History of Britain: that part especially now called England*, betrayed his

---

52. Of course, the religious pursuit of perfect virtue is the pursuit of an impossibility, at least in the sublunary world. But the religious person understands this; the doctrine of Original Sin makes him well aware of it. Moral perfection is aimed at not in the expectation of reaching it this side of paradise, but to spur the effort to be better than one would otherwise be. In my own case, I believe that politeness is a social virtue, but this does not mean that I am myself always polite. Like everyone else I am a fallen creature. But this in turn does not mean that I do not really believe in politeness as a social virtue, much less that it is not in actual fact a social virtue. Only if I were *never* or *very seldom* polite, and did not value politeness in others, would it be reasonable to doubt the sincerity of my belief. Hazlitt has an interesting essay on the distinctions between cant, true belief, and hypocrisy: distinctions that are often missed.

disappointment that the unity and sense of purpose that infused the parliamentary forces during the Civil War dissipated almost at once:

> But when once the superficiall zeal and popular fumes that acted their New Magistracy were cool'd and spent in them, strait everyone betook himself (setting the Commonwealth behind, his privat ends before) to doe as his own profit or ambition ledd him. Then was justice delay'd, and soon after deny'd: spight and favour determin'd all: hence faction, thence treachery, both at home and in the field; ev'ry where wrong, and oppression: foul and horrid deeds committed daily, or maintain'd, in secret, or in open. . . . Their Votes and Ordinances, which men looked should have contain'd the repealing of bad laws, and the immediate constitution of better, resounded with nothing els, but new Impositions, Taxes, Excises; yearly, monthly, weekly. Not to reckon the Offices, Gifts, and Preferments bestow'd and shar'd among themselves.

The pork-barrel is nothing new, then; and in fact Milton's outrage, typical of the disappointed utopian dreamer, is the product, surely, of a deficient knowledge of human nature, in his case caused by too great an attention to books and too little to men.

To speak of my own case, I feel very English, despite my mongrel origins, a feeling that, according to my French relations by marriage, has some objective correlatives, not all of them to be deprecated. But I certainly don't feel only English, and indeed (being a doctor) feel more in common with almost any member of the medical profession from anywhere in the world than with many of my nation, my nation now specializing in the breeding up of charmless drunken screaming vulgarians.

THE IMPORTANCE OF NATIONAL IDENTITY

Nevertheless, where political questions are concerned, it is probable that in the majority of people national identity (at least in most of the world) is now the strongest, deepest, and most fundamental aspect of their identity to which politicians can appeal, though Islamism is making inroads into this. Socialists spent the decades before the First World War speaking of international working-class solidarity, but promptly voted war credits to their respective national governments everywhere when asked to do so. Proletarian internationalism after the Second World War was a ridiculous euphemism for Soviet domination, which existed only among the satraps of whoever was in power in the Soviet Union at the time. The idea that Pole would be reconciled with Russian by the forcible inculcation of Marx's inversion of the Hegelian dialectic has only to be expressed for its absurdity to become evident. To adapt slightly a famous Marxian dictum (one that is true and profound[53]), identities can be forged, but not in any way men choose.

It does not follow from the fact that identities are often deliberately and self-consciously forged, therefore, that it would be possible to forge a European identity, a Europeanism of the heart, as it were. But let us suppose for a moment that it were; would it be either necessary or desirable?

If you ask someone who is in favor of the European project for his reasons, why he thinks that national sovereignty should be reduced, and supranational powers increased, and why Belgians, Romanians, Estonians, and Portuguese should feel deeply something more in common than heretofore, he will almost certainly reply, "To avoid war" or "To secure peace."

On this view, the natural state of European man, his default setting as it were, is war. For this there appears to be quite a lot of evidence, historically speaking. There have indeed been an awful lot of wars in Europe, almost as many as coffee beans in Brazil. It is not even as if all of them were minor, before the First and Second World Wars. The Thirty Years War, for example, resulted in the

---

53. *Men make their own history, but not in any way they choose.* Oddly enough, this has no bearing on the question of freedom and determinism. The fact that I cannot jump to the moon does not mean that there is not an infinite number and variety of movements that I can make.

deaths of a third of the population of Germany. Of Napoleon I will not speak, for fear of offending my French wife.

Nor can it really be said that friendships between peoples have grown up spontaneously since the end of the last war, or that traditionally hostile national feelings have warmed into affection. The term *anglo-saxon*, I have noticed, is not one of approbation or affection when used in French newspapers; Albion is still *perfide*, and *les rosbifs* are disgusting (they often are, of course). British tabloid newspapers appeal to the prejudices of their readership and maintain their circulations by xenophobic jibes against the French, alluding to such alleged facts as their reduced consumption of soap; and when English play French football teams, the English crowd tends to chant, "If it weren't for us, you'd all be speaking Kraut." This is not exactly a manifestation of pan-European solidarity, at least in the affective sphere.

PERSISTENT ANIMOSITIES

I have never in France heard anyone say anything good about Germany or Germans (their cars excepted), despite more than half a century of official friendship and alliance. My wife and I had landed at Frankfurt Airport, her first time ever in Germany. The first words addressed to her by a German in Germany were "Vy are you so late?" uttered by a stern Lufthansa air hostess as we hurried on to an aircraft for a connecting flight. "*Sale boche!*" were the words that came spontaneously to my wife's lips, though other, non-national, insults were available to her.

On the Queen's birthday in Holland, the national holiday, cars bearing German license plates are often still scratched or vandalized in other ways, and in general it is advisable for Germans with cars to retreat discreetly over the border for the day. No doubt this phenomenon is lessening, but that it should exist at all is hardly a tribute to neighborly good feeling.

In Belgium, the Walloons and the Flemish are hardly on speaking terms. Apart from Brussels, you would not know that Belgium, officially, is a bilingual state. In Wallonia, there is not a single sign in Flemish; in Flanders, within a yard of the border, there is not a single sign in French. In Flanders, people refused to speak French, and preferred to address us in English; indeed, the young people now learn English in preference to French, which they do not know and (which is an appalling thing) do not wish to know. I had great difficulty in Flanders finding a French-language newspaper, let alone a bookshop that sold books in French.

No doubt this can all be explained perfectly well historically. For most of its existence, Belgium has been dominated, economically, politically, and culturally, by its French-speaking minority, but now the boot is firmly on the other foot. The Flemish are two-thirds of the population, and far the more prosperous. The traditional industries of Wallonia—coal-mining and steel-making—have collapsed, leaving mass unemployment and dependence on state handouts, paid for, of course, by the newly prosperous and flourishing Flemish. (Such, at any rate, is the belief of the Flemish, who argue, no doubt self-interestedly but not necessarily wrongly, that a withdrawal of their subsidies from the Walloons would do them good. The Socialist Party, which runs Wallonia like a fiefdom, does not agree, since its power depends entirely upon the distribution of those subsidies.)

However historically explicable the disagreements of the Walloons and the Flemish might be, they are certainly not a tribute to the brotherly feelings of all European people, or of their instinctive sympathy with one another, let alone a feeling of common identity and perhaps destiny.

If this is the case, argue those in favor of the European project (the construction of what amounts to a super-state, reducing formerly national governments to the status of municipalities), really hostile and war-like emotions between peoples could easily be aroused again. The nearer they are to the surface, the more imperative it is that they should be constrained with hoops of international supranational institutions. If not, war could break out at any time. It is to accept on a European scale what Bertrand Russell believed, as he wrote in his essay *The Future of Mankind*, to be the case on a world scale:

[It] is [not] reasonable to hope that, if nothing drastic is done, wars will nevertheless not occur. They have always occurred from time to time, and obviously will break out again sooner or later unless mankind adopt some system that makes them impossible. But the only such system is a single government with a monopoly of armed force.[54]

THE CAUSES OF PEACE

The proof of the wisdom of the expanding supranational European authority is that there has been no war in Europe for the past sixty years, at least between members of the European Union. (Of course there was the small matter of France's Algerian war, which cost up to a million lives; Britain has had conflicts with Argentina, Serbia, and Iraq; and a kaleidoscopic cast of European nations has sent troops to Iraq and Afghanistan. But the point still holds: there has been no armed conflict between members of the European Union.)

This argument is a deeply pessimistic one, since it depends for its force on the supposition that, had it not been for what is now called the European Union, the European nations would have been at each other's throats again. This can be neither proved nor disproved; neither can its opposite, of course. The argument can be scanned only for plausibility.

---

54. Russell's essay, published in book form in 1950, is a perfect illustration of the perils of political prediction. It goes without saying that he was not a stupid man; and (which is not always the same thing) he sometimes showed the greatest good sense, for example early spotting in Lenin, whom he met in Russia when he visited, a monster of a new kind. Here are his three possibilities for the state of the world by the year 2000, one of which he said was more or less *inevitable*:

I. The end of human life, perhaps of all life on our planet.
II. A reversion to barbarism after a catastrophic diminution of the population of the globe.
III. A unification of the world under a single government, possessing a monopoly of all the major weapons of war.

Admittedly, Russell said that one of the three above *must* happen (my emphasis), but it is difficult to see what it was that, in the event, prevented the predicted outcome.

The first thing to note is that many of the countries were never likely to attack anyone anyway. One can hardly conceive of Luxembourg declaring war on Italy, or Lithuania on Portugal. Therefore, at the heart of the argument is the relationship between France and Germany: only a war between them might drag Greece into conflict with Finland, if each of them took different sides.

We are therefore asked to believe that without the giant bureaucratic apparatus now in place in Brussels—that without bureaucratic pronouncements on such subjects as the size bananas should be and the illegality of using pounds, ounces, and inches as units of measurement in Britain and Ireland, to say nothing of scores of thousands of other pronouncements—France and Germany would sooner or later go to war again (which they now will not, the question of the size of bananas having been settled to everyone's satisfaction). Moreover, since no one really believes that it would be France that would attack Germany rather than the other way round, it boils down to this: that without a vast European apparatus, the Hun would get up to his tricks again.

But would he? To assume that he would means that there subsists in him some kind of unchangeable essence, incapable of change, and certainly not from learning from experience. The Bundesrepublik, on this view, is only the Third Reich waiting to burst forth from its democratic integument.

There have been people who believed this, though not very respectable ones. It was a point of view that the Soviet Union long tried to peddle and persuade people of. Its original argument was that there were a lot of Nazis employed by the new state (there were none, of course, left in East Germany), which was therefore a continuation of the Third Reich by other means. It tried to maintain that West Germany's limited re-armament was the first stage towards a revanchist war. It argued that West Germany's capitalist economic system was inherently imperialist and would, by the logic of capitalism itself, seek markets and sources of raw materials by warlike means. So far, at any rate, all these arguments have been refuted by experience, and I see no reason to suppose that future experience will confirm them. If anything, Germany has been an almost exemplary social-democratic state, solicitous of the rights of its citizens, pacific in its policies, and almost too shy to exercise its economic muscle.

The Baader-Meinhof gang claimed that West Germany was a neo-Nazi state also, and justified their violence and criminality on that ground. (Not surprisingly, they received assistance from East Germany.) As has become all too typical of western youth, they mistook their personal angst for a universal political cause. True, they were in a difficult and in some respects unenviable and uncomfortable situation (about the historical burden of which I shall have more to say soon); they lived in a free and liberal society whose previous generation had participated, with varying degrees of enthusiasm, and quite recently, in one of the worst episodes in human history. They could not know who around them was who, and who had done what. Instead of drawing a cautious and careful lesson from this, however, they drew the most reckless one possible, no doubt to justify their desire for transcendent historical significance and their taste for violent action.

From any serious point of view, however, the idea that the new Bundesrepublik was simply the continuation of Nazi Germany by other means was not worthy of examination, any more than it would be worth sending a space probe to examine the question of whether the moon is made of green cheese.

GERMAN SELF-DEPRECATION

One does still, however, meet Germans who mistrust themselves, or rather their fellow-countrymen, so greatly that they see reversions to (supposed) type lurking everywhere, including in situations that others would find completely innocent. I had a startling example of this when I had dinner in Germany with a man, not born until ten years after the end of the war, who ran his family forestry business. He decided it would be good for business to have a company mission statement (or perhaps bad for business not to have one), and called a meeting to decide what it should be. Someone suggested *Holz mit Stolz*—Forestry with Pride—and there followed a lengthy discussion as to whether this signified the beginning of the slippery slope to . . . well, it didn't have to be specified where, everyone knew the destination.

Taken seriously, this meant that no German should ever again be allowed pride in what he did; but since so rigorous a view, which is against human nature, was likely to irritate and produce a counter-reaction, eschewing pride was as likely to lead to the beginning of the slippery slope as its adoption. In other words, the slippery slope beckoned however any German behaved.

The fear of Germany is by now ridiculous, and anyone who sees the visage of Frederick the Great, let alone that of Hitler, lurking behind the visage of Angela Merkel, needs not so much refutation by argument as an appointment with a psychiatrist. There never was the faintest prospect of renewed armed conflict between France and Germany after the end of the Second World War, and there was therefore no need of any structure to prevent it.

COMMON CURRENCY AS A SOURCE
OF NATIONAL ANTAGONISM

Paradoxically, too close a union between disparate national states could easily lead to conflict where none existed before. Monetary union could, in certain circumstances, some of which appear now to be eventuating, leave weak states of the union with an unpleasant choice between international and domestic strife. For example, Greece joined the European monetary union with the help of statistical legerdemain—precisely the kind of legerdemain that anyone would expect of any government that had to present itself in a good light to others in order to pursue its ends (I make no cheap jibes about national characteristics). Membership of the monetary union leaves a small state like Greece with little room for maneuver when a crisis occurs: it cannot, within the rules, expand its deficit too far, and it cannot devalue its currency to make its exports, produced inefficiently, more attractive to foreign buyers. If it were to try to leave the union, and reinstitute the national currency, there would not only be an immediate and colossal flight of capital, and an end for quite a long time to foreign investment, but the country would still have a large, Euro-denominated debt to pay (it already has to pay 2.5 percent per annum more interest on its debt in Euros than Germany, such is the perceived risk of its default), and it would have to face the wrath of its European partners, many of whom are in similar boats, and who might similarly be forced before long to leave the monetary union, bringing the whole edifice crashing down, with goodness knows what repercussions everywhere. The only solution for Greece to avoid conflict with other countries would be to reduce its level of consumption to meet its financial obligations, but this is unlikely to appeal to a population that already believes that it is unfairly and unjustly impoverished by corrupt and venal politicians who have sliced up the economy like a cake for them and their friends to eat at their leisure. Greece is oversupplied with precisely the most dangerous kind of people in situations of social conflict: unemployed young university graduates who believe themselves to have been deprived of the opportunities to which their education entitles them and who, when thwarted, adopt the most extreme ideologies.[55] If Greece had never entered the monetary union, it seems to me likely that its dilemmas would have been rather less acute, and its room for maneuver larger.[56]

At any rate, it seems to me clear that there is no good argument for a European super-state from the need to prevent war, and there is some reason to suppose that such a state would actually increase the likelihood of conflict, since it is unlikely that the advanced or provident countries of Europe will want to go on forever paying for the backward or improvident ones, nor is it very likely that in

---

55. Here it is important to point out that what counts is not the absolute standard of living that people have, nor the difference between the present and the past, but the difference between what they have and what they expect. Anyone looking at pictures of the Greek riots in 2009 will—or ought to have been—struck by how singularly healthy, well-fed, and well-dressed the rioters looked. Greece, indeed, has one of the highest life expectancies in the world. The generation of rioters was, in fact, the best-off Greeks by far who have ever existed. But no one with a knowledge of himself and his rages, let alone of human nature in general, would expect that fact to exert a restraining effect upon the self-righteous vandalism of the rioters.

56. I am not here making any definite predictions: to do so after having ridiculed a prediction by Bertrand Russell would be presumptuous. I speak only of plausibilities.

the foreseeable future the countries will equalize in the matter of providence and the wisdom of their economic management. Like the ant in La Fontaine's fable *"La cigale et la fourmi"* (a short poem that contains all the most valuable principles of political economy), to whom the cicada, having sung all summer, applies for a loan when she finds she has nothing to eat in the winter, the provident countries will eventually return the following answer to the improvident ones:

> *Vous chantiez? J'en suis fort aise:*
> Eh bien! Dansez maintenant.

> So you sang? I'm very glad.
> Well, now you can dance!

Then all hell will break loose.

WHAT IS IT REALLY ALL ABOUT?

It seems to me very unlikely that the founders of the European Union, who after all were worldly and intelligent men, really believed that without it war would break out in Europe once again, like a recurrence of an infectious disease from which there is only partial and temporary immunity. The real motives must therefore have been different: What were they?

Real motives, as against declared ones, are always a matter of conjecture, and cannot finally be proved to have operated. Like orders for genocide, they are rarely committed to paper, so we can only speculate as to what they might be. Demonstrative proof is lacking, but if we thought only about those things about which such proof were available, our minds would be empty most of the time. So here goes.

France and Germany were the key powers, the unmoved movers of the project, as it were, but their motives, though interlocking and complementary, were different.

The Germans had an identity and a past that they badly needed to forget. From having been the most rabid and ruthless nationalists in the history of the world, they wanted henceforth to blend into a background, into a kind of *macédoine de nations*, a salad of nations. Only thus could they prove that they had really changed, that they no longer believed themselves to be the only world-historical nation, that they were no longer the purveyors of the jackboot to the face of other nations (to change the metaphor slightly). I remember once meeting a stranger in a cafe, and when in the course of the conversation I asked him where he was from, he replied, "I am a European." It was clear from his accent that he was German; I repeated my question, "Yes, but where are you from?" "I am a European," he insisted, as if he were one of those products that now carry the label "Made in the E.U." I doubt very much whether anyone but a German would have answered thus.

The French had a different motive. Their country, like all the countries in Europe except Russia, had been reduced to secondary status in the scale of world power. They were realistic enough to understand that there was nothing they could do about this: their territory simply was too small, as was their population, to be able to compete with the United States or the Soviet Union (as was). But, like General de Gaulle, they had a certain idea of France, amongst which was its world importance and significance for the whole of humanity.[57]

The way in which the circle could be squared was by close alliance with Germany. The energy, intelligence, and single-mindedness with which the Germans rebuilt their economy after the war was soon obvious for all to see (to this day, Germany remains the largest exporter of goods in the world). France could appropriate

---

57. Cf. the saying that every man has two homelands, his own and France. This is not wholly ridiculous: the Dutch and Germans have another saying, "To live as God in France;" more than half a million British have bought homes there (and yet more would if they could); and France is by far the most popular tourist destination in the world. There is no single field of important human endeavor in which the French have not excelled and contributed vastly more than is proportionate to their territory or population, to say nothing of their famous *savoir vivre*. Recent American anti-French feeling was both crude and stupid, no better than reflexive anti-Americanism.

the *Wirtschaftswunder* to remain of world importance, because the Germans, thanks to their recent history, would remain politically passive for a long time to come. Eventually, because of world developments, even union with Germany was not sufficient; for Europe to count at all at the high table of world power, it would have to expand. This carried the risk of dilution of French influence within the union it created, but then circles were never very easy to square.

Why and how has a union that was created to serve interlocking German and French purposes come to have a life of its own, and to command the allegiance of all the politicians—except a few mavericks of no account—of the whole of Europe? This despite the absurdities of the organization, and the fact that on many occasions it acts against the national interests of the countries that compose it.

EUROPEAN UNION AS A PENSION FUND

The answer, I think, is obvious: the European Union is like a giant pension fund for defunct politicians, who either cannot get elected in their own countries or are tired of the struggle to do so. It is a way for politicians to remain important and powerful, at the center of a web of patronage, after their defeat or loss of willingness to expose themselves to the rigors of the electoral process. One of the characteristics of modern political life is its professionalization, such that it attracts mainly the kind of people with so great an avidity for power and self-importance that they do not mind very much the humiliations of the public exposure to which they are inevitably subjected.[58] They are increasingly like Lloyd George, the British Prime Minister, of whom John Maynard Keynes was

---

58. This explains why, in Britain, politicians have increasingly little sense of honor. There is no such thing any longer as resigning for good in disgrace, having been caught with fingers in the till, or some such. Resignation lasts only until the sensation caused by the revelation of wrong-doing blows over, and everyone, distracted by a thousand other sensations, has forgotten all about it. Then the politician comes creeping back into office. Brazen and thick-skinned, he does not feel disgraced, only inconvenienced. At best, he *acts* as if he felt disgraced, but only for as short a time as possible, and only for effect.

once asked what he thought about when he was alone in a room. "When Lloyd George is alone in a room," replied Keynes, "there's nobody there." It seems that there are more and more people like this, who derive their sense of themselves as truly existing only in front of an audience, preferably of millions.

No one bites the hand that feeds it, or even that might feed it at some time in the foreseeable future, especially as handsomely as the European hand feeds those who play ball with it. You can spot a feeder at the European trough (to change the metaphor once again) a mile off: having for a long time viewed the world exclusively through the windows of an official limousine, having lunched and dined heavily for many years (never at his own expense, of course), and having developed a special *langue de bois* in which streams of grammatically formed verbiage are carefully studded with words of positive connotation that makes it difficult to argue against him, he has developed the gray, immobile, slab-faced countenance of former members of the Soviet Politburo. Alas, it seems that there are a large number of volunteers— mainly mediocrities, of course—for this kind of life. It seems to them eminently preferable to earning a living.

Hence even those who start out with a predilection against the European project soon find, after an expense claim or two, that it is not so bad after all. And what career politician could be altogether against an organization of politicians and bureaucrats whose accounts have never, ever been signed off by the auditors as being correct? For politicians to abolish such a delightful organization would be like a federation of butchers voting for compulsory vegetarianism.

8.

WHY ARE WE LIKE THIS (III)?

Besides a virtual subscription to the excellent restaurants of Brussels, paid for by someone else, one of the great attractions of the European project—the development of a super-state, the equal of the United States or China—is of course power. The power that is desired is not that which is sufficient for self-determination, to live as far as possible as one pleases, but to push other people about, to dominate them, to loom large in their calculations, to make their decisions for them. This is rarely far from the minds of those who support the project who feel humiliated and irritated that, having ruled the world roost for so long, Europe has been reduced to world insignificance (in the matter of power) just at the very moment that they themselves have achieved office and would have been so much more important if they had been born a hundred years earlier.

An excellent example of this is contained in an article in the liberal British newspaper *The Guardian* for March 26, 2009, by the political commentator Timothy Garton Ash. The headline is indicative of the tone: "One great power will be absent from the London G20 summit. Guess who?" The burden of the argument is that world power is not only desirable but vital for our well-being because "If we carry on like this [i.e. disunited], we Europeans will have chosen not to hang together—we will end up hanging separately." The obvious consideration that, if we all hang together and choose the wrong policy (at a time when, truth to tell, no one can be sure what the right policy is), then we will all hang together, does not seem to have occurred to him. People who normally go into dithyrambs at the very mention of diversity do not seem to realize that here is an occasion when diversity might actually, by experimentation, have very important lessons to teach. Disunity might be more of an advantage than a disadvantage. Only an obsession with power as a good in itself could have prevented an intelligent man like Garton Ash from seeing this.

At any rate, it seems to me unlikely that the desire of the European political elite for world power and influence will so communicate itself to and be shared by any considerable part of the population of the countries of Europe that a genuinely European sense of identity will develop beyond its current very rudimentary and lukewarm state. The enthusiasm for Europe will remain strictly a thing of the mind rather than of the heart,[59] and as soon as problems arise, as they have recently arisen (to put it mildly), the leaders will react according to their national interest. There was widespread indignation reported among various European officials soon after the demand for cars declined drastically when the French President, Nicolas Sarkozy, in effect encouraged the French carmaker Renault

---

59. A proof of this was an address by the British Prime Minister, Mr. Brown, to the European Parliament. "It is thanks to the work of all of you and the generations whose work we continue that we enjoy a Europe of peace and unity which will truly rank among the finest of human achievements." He continued, "So I stand here today proud to be British and proud to be European representing a country that does not see itself as an island beside Europe but a country at the center of Europe, not in Europe's slipstream but firmly in its mainstream." As if this were not all quite bad enough already, he went on: "So let it be said of us that at the worst of times, in the deepest of downturns, we kept to our faith in the future and together we reshaped and renewed the world order for our times." This sounds like a man with Asperger's Syndrome trying to imitate someone with normal human feelings, or perhaps only an apparatchik trying to be grandiloquent. I doubt that anyone would risk very much on behalf of the Europe of Mr. Brown's speech.

to repatriate such production as was still required from other European countries to France. This, they said, was against the European rules: Renault, a French company, was supposed, especially if it was in receipt of state aid, to site its factories according to commercial and not to political or patriotic criteria.

DOING THEIR BEST FOR THEIR ELECTORATES

The case illustrated the contradiction at the heart of the European Union: it requires obedience to rules that had had no democratic oversight, let alone sanction, and to which no one can wholeheartedly subscribe (just as the European Bank could, in theory, set an interest rate that conformed to no country's economic needs). Mr. Sarkozy was elected president of France, however; he had an electoral mandate to protect and promote the interests of France and nowhere else. Whether or not his encouragement of Renault to repatriate jobs to France and concentrate redundancies elsewhere really did serve the interests of France in the long run is no doubt a question that is susceptible to more than one answer; at any rate, I can certainly think of more than one way of answering the question; but I think it likely that the great majority of his countrymen, his electors, approved of it. If Mr. Sarkozy had been indifferent as to the location in which Renault laid off its workforce, he would have been open to a number of charges, including a lack of patriotism and an undemocratic refusal to respect the wishes and feelings of his voters. Those voters did not think, "Those poor Slovak car workers formerly employed by Renault, they are fellow Europeans about whose welfare I am as worried as that of my fellow-Frenchmen, and therefore I think that redundancies might as well be in France. Indeed, it would be better that they were, because French unemployment benefits are so much more generous than Slovak ones, and therefore the sum of European suffering would be less if the redundancies were in France." No doubt there could be found someone somewhere in France who thinks like this; but I doubt whether a single person could be found there who *feels* like it.

In other words, in situations in which hard choices have to be made, decisions made genuinely in the interest of Europe rather than of any of the particular countries that make it up will do violence to the real and spontaneous feelings of many people in those countries. And this will create, ultimately, a rich breeding ground for the kind of resentments with which we in Europe are already more than sufficiently familiar. In the early days of the recession, there were wildcat strikes in various parts of Britain (for some time the most open economy in Europe) against the employment of labor from the European Union in oil refineries and on construction sites, though there is supposed to be a perfectly free labor market throughout the union. When there is full employment and an expanding economy, the freedom of labor is not a problem, beyond the occasional friction caused by the proximity of groups of people who are strangers to one another; but the moment an economy comes again to be seen as a zero-sum game, in which my share is your deprivation and *vice versa*, deeply xenophobic passions are likely to flourish.[60]

Even in the best of times, through which we do not appear currently to be living, the appeal of the European project, of a superstate to rival that of the United States or China, would not be sufficient to generate a pan-European consciousness, that is to say a lasting loyalty that replaces current national loyalties and feelings. In hard times, when economic life seems more of a struggle than it has been for years or decades, the chances of such a loyalty developing are nil.

AN EXPERIMENT AGAINST REALITY

Against this elementary reality, the European plan of dividing up even countries such as England into "regions," with regional

---

60. I am not saying that a modern economy ever is in reality a zero-sum game, only that it is more likely to appear as such during times of recession, depression, and slump. It is perhaps asking more of a redundant car worker than is psychologically realistic to believe anything else; and in politics, what people actually do believe is as important as, or more important than, what they ought to believe if they were wholly rational beings.

assemblies that will supposedly serve to reduce national feeling and thus advance the cause of what one might call European federative centralization, or (to use a more emotive term) *Gleichschaltung*, is bound to fail. But even schemes that are bound to fail can cause a lot of havoc before they do.

9.

WHY ARE WE LIKE THIS (IV)?

We have seen that neither real religion nor the secular religion of the Founding Fathers that the Unites States has been able from its inception to propagate and instill in its citizenry can provide for European man the sense of personal transcendence that seems to be necessary for a fulfilled life. What of ordinary patriotism? In a country in which patriotism is widespread, even the humblest of citizens may share some portion of the pride. A man may be only a postman, but he is helping the wheels of a great country to turn.

PATRIOTISM AND ITS DISCONTENTS

Ordinary patriotism can be promoted by a number of situations or factors. The greatness or importance of a country can promote it; a sense of national oppression, danger, or enmity can also do it; or a feeling that the country is in some way special or unique can do it. Needless to say, patriotism when excessive can become jingoism, arrogance, xenophobia, and belligerence; self-respect becomes self-conceit, and love of homeland becomes hatred of everywhere else. Like all other virtues, patriotism when carried to excess becomes a vice; but that does not mean that patriotism is incompatible with respect for others.

Dr. Johnson's famous remark, that patriotism is the last refuge of the scoundrel, is often quoted as an argument against patriotism,[61] but its sense is misunderstood. There was, of course, no man more fervently English than the doctor: indeed, he is often taken to be the epitome of Englishman. What he was saying was not that patriotism was wrong, but that a scoundrel will not scruple to proclaim it to advance his dishonest argument or scheme.

Nevertheless, patriotism had generally had a bad press in Europe for the last half century or more, being considered the handmaiden of historical disaster. Bertrand Russell sneered at it on the grounds that, for most people, the country to which they were attached was an accident of birth, the assumption being that one should enthuse over only what one has freely chosen oneself, without the intervention of fortuitous circumstances (as if there were, or could be, any such choices). Here is his characterization of patriotism in his essay *An Outline of Intellectual Rubbish*:

> If he is an Englishman, he thinks of Shakespeare and Milton, or of Newton and Darwin, or of Nelson and Wellington, according to his temperament. If he is a Frenchman, he congratulates himself on the fact that for centuries France has led the world in culture, fashions, and cookery. If he is a Russian, he reflects that he belongs to the only nation which is truly international. If he is a Yugoslav, he boasts of his nation's pigs; if a native of the Principality of Monaco, he boasts of leading the world in the matter of gambling.

Thus is patriotism ridiculed, though one cannot help but notice that the depiction by Russell (an Englishman) of English patrio-

---

61. Do citations provide arguments or evidence, or are they mere appeals to authority? At any rate, we all use them to bolster what we say.

tism seems somewhat more serious in its exciting causes than that of other nations. It would, perhaps, be a cheap jibe to observe that Russell's adoption of an empiricist philosophy might have had something to do with the land of his birth: had he been born elsewhere, he might have been an idealist or even an animist. It goes without saying that this consideration does not affect one's assessment of the worth of that philosophy.

How, asked Archbishop Paley of Edward Gibbon's account of the rise and triumph of Christianity, does one refute a sneer? I have travelled in many countries and have found reasons for national pride in almost all of them; I have even become patriotic on behalf of some of them, without in the slightest losing attachment to my own native land and culture (deeply debased as it may now have become).

But the arguments in Europe against patriotism are compelling, though not necessarily strong. They derive, of course, from its history.

Nothing is easier than to present the history of Europe as that of war and man-made catastrophe. The very clever American author Claire Berlinski did precisely that in her book *Menace in Europe*, in which she gave a list of European wars that covered a full, quite closely printed page. She begins the list with these words:

> [The European brotherhood] is all very touching, considering that it replaces century upon century of unmitigated slaughter and butchery among European peoples, a tradition of virtually uninterrupted warfare since the sack of Rome.

NOTHING BUT-ISM

The word "unmitigated" implies that, in the history of Europe, there is nothing but war and massacre. And if this is so, there is nothing to be proud of, nothing worth preserving, in the culture or tradition that gave rise to this war and massacre. Indeed, the culture and tradition are of war and massacre, and nothing besides.

As a factual statement, of course, this is absurd. It is not necessary, indeed it is hardly possible, to deny the part that internecine warfare has played in European history, but to suggest that there has been nothing else of any significance in it is merely silly, like suggesting that the history of the United States is nothing but the history of its military interventions in Latin America. Many of the wars listed on the page affected most of Europe not at all; if war and massacre had been the overwhelming and unmitigated experience of Europeans, it is difficult to see how they could have created all that they did create.

Of course, importance is not a natural quality; it is a quality that an ascribing mind affixes to facts, rather than a quality inhering in the facts themselves. If someone says that he finds in European history nothing of importance except its wars, he is entitled to do so; perhaps he considers the absence of war to be the highest good. But this leaves it open to someone else to say that he finds in European history nothing of importance but artistic glory, or agricultural progress, or whatever else his enthusiasm may light upon, disregarding the wars as epiphenomena of no real account. Nothing is easier than to write a history of a human endeavor, portraying it as a succession of crime and folly.[62]

PROBLEMS IN AND WITH THE PAST

Whatever the correct and balanced approach to history might be, there can be little doubt that Europe now has a problem with its history, and that this has deep, if sometimes subliminal, effects.

---

62. "It is a curious and painful fact"—wrote Russell in *An Outline of Intellectual Rubbish*—"that almost all the completely futile treatments that have been believed in during the long history of medical folly have been such as caused acute suffering to the patient." Recently, I reviewed a history of medicine composed of doctors' innumerable errors and absurdities. This is perfectly legitimate, and indeed instructive as a warning against too eager adoption of outré ideas, provided that the history is not presented as the one and only, the *true*, history of medicine.

It has gone from a confident and overweening view of itself, to a miserabilist one (which, however, is not, as we shall see, without its self-aggrandizing aspects). And this is not because of its "virtually uninterrupted warfare since the sack of Rome," which was perfectly compatible for long periods with the greatest self-esteem (incidentally, I disregard the question of whether the history of Asia or Mesoamerica is any the less the history of warfare than is Europe's) but because of events in the twentieth century.

For a hundred years before the outbreak of the First World War, Europe had experienced no pan-European war. There had been wars aplenty, of course, a list of which would fill a page, especially if colonial conflicts were included. Still, the era seemed one of overall peace, progress, and increasing plenty, all of which came to seem "natural," as if they were ordained in the nature of European civilization itself, which accorded itself the highest accolade as the peak of human achievement.

The self-confidence that permitted Europeans to colonize and rule much of the rest of the world was shattered by the First World War. There had no doubt been premonitions of a crisis of confidence in artistic and intellectual circles before the war, the Newtonian worldview had sundered, and so vast a conflict as that war can hardly have come about without any intellectual or material preparation for it. Still, the depiction of peace, rationality, material advance, increasing comfort, and refinement in Stefan Zweig's memoir, *The World of Yesterday*, rings true. Europe was the center of the world, morally and intellectually, and in its own opinion, deservedly (and permanently) so.

The means by which the First World War destroyed this self-confidence were not quite as straightforward as sometimes maintained. Most people think that the war, which killed and maimed millions, was intrinsically senseless and came to be seen as such at the time. This led, not surprisingly, to complete disillusionment with the leaders who, through sheer incompetence, blindness, and folly, had brought it about; and furthermore, that the culture of which this war was a manifestation must be a worthless one too.

This is not the place to decide whether the war was, or was not, "really" senseless.[63] Like their importance, the sense of facts is not in the facts themselves, but in the mind that assesses them. Whether the Germans really were trying to secure world-domination, and if so whether this was the real reason Britain, France, and Russia went to war with it, is a question for historians. What is important is whether the population of Europe saw the war as "senseless."

At least to the victors, the war did not seem self-evidently senseless, and disillusionment was not immediate. The war memorials to be found everywhere in France are tributes to loss, but not to meaninglessness. The soldiers really did die for France, or so almost everyone supposed; in Britain, my next-door neighbor, who collects coins and medals, showed me some First World War service medals for those who survived the war, with an athletic (and naked) young man upon a horse, wielding a sword as if he were a latter-day St. George about to slay a dragon. One of the medals bore the inscription "The War to Save Civilization." I doubt that these medals were greeted solely by hollow laughter; for one thing, they would hardly have been preserved so carefully if they had been. And browsing in a bookshop recently, I found a book published in 1918 with the title *The Romance of War Inventions*. It was an attempt to interest boys in science by explaining how shells, mortars, tanks, and so forth had been developed and how they worked. By the time of its publication, millions had already been killed, and surely no one in Britain could by that time not have known someone who had been killed or at least someone whose child or brother or parent had been killed. It seems to me unlikely that such a publication would have seen the light of day in an atmosphere of generalized cynicism about the war.

---

63. At press conferences at which senior British policemen make their first comment on a murder, they often say "This was a particularly vicious and senseless [or unnecessary] murder"—as if there were sensible and necessary murders.

A CHANGE OF MEANING

The version of the First World War that is now almost universally accepted as "true" is that of the disillusioned writers, male and female, of the late 1920s and 1930s. The war, according this version, was about nothing at all and was caused by blundering politicians, prolonged by stupid generals and lauded by patriotic fools. Irrespective of the justification of this view—and surely there is something in it—some of the people who propagated it did not accurately represent their own feelings about the war at the time. Vera Brittain, the prominent pacifist who wrote a memoir entitled *Testament of Youth*, published in 1933, wrote that her brother, and others like him, had been killed "in order to save the face of a Foreign Secretary who had committed his country to an armed policy without consulting it beforehand," without mentioning that it was she who had encouraged her brother to join up in the first place, against the opposition of their father, and that, the day before Britain declared war, she had written in her diary "the great fear now is that our bungling Government will declare England's neutrality." She claimed in her memoir that she was so traumatized by what she had seen as an auxiliary just behind the front that, after the war was over, she was unable to enjoy her time at Oxford: when her personal papers demonstrate quite the reverse, that she had a jolly time. The most famous memoirists of the war similarly revised their experiences, and one is inclined to forget that verses such as the following:

> All that a man might ask hast thou given me, England,
> Yet grant thou one thing more:
> That now when envious foes would spoil thy splendour,
> Unversed in arms, a dreamer such as I,
> May in thy ranks be deemed not all unworthy,
> England, for thee to die . . .

were actually far more numerous, and for a time more influential on the popular imagination, than the anti-war poets. André Maurois's classic fictional account of his time as a French army liaison officer on the western front with the British army, *Les silences du Colonel Bramble*, written and published towards the end of the war, certainly does not convey any sense of futility or absurdity, despite all the horrors Maurois must have seen and heard about. There is no reason to think that Maurois was not perfectly sincere in his admiration for the members of the British army whom he depicted (one of whom, Doctor O'Grady, the regiment's medical officer, was an Irishman without a hint of Irish nationalism) at the time.

In other words, the disillusionment that set in was probably not a direct and spontaneous consequence of the war, but the result of intellectual reflection upon its meaning. This is not to say that it was incorrect, or any more incorrect than the view that the war had been fought to save civilization; there is no reason why reconsideration of events should not lead to different conclusions about their meaning from those at first entertained.[64] What is bad is not the change of opinion, but the lack of acknowledgment of a change of opinion, the pretense that the new assessment of the war was the assessment made of it at the time. This means that the memoirs are essentially propaganda for a certain view, however compelling they and it might appear to be.

But if they were propaganda, they were very successful propaganda, and within a very short time this propaganda established

---

64. An instance in my own case is the following. When, at the end of 1990, President Ceausescu of Romania was overthrown, and he and his wife were executed after a summary trial, I, who had been in Romania shortly before his overthrow and seen the oppressiveness of his rule, felt a kind of euphoria. But a cousin of mine, whose opinion I do not always respect, pointed out what was obviously true, that the trial had been unfair and unjust; that one of the charges, genocide, was simply ludicrous; and that people, however bad they were, should not be taken to a courtyard and there shot as if they were stray dogs. She was obviously right; and I now feel ashamed at having enthused over the death of the horrible couple. Moreover, the overthrow turned out to have been more of a coup d'état, the outcome of a conspiracy installing Ceausescu's former henchmen in power, than a genuinely popular revolt—which is not to say that he was not a genuinely hated, and hateful, figure.

itself as an indisputable orthodoxy. Between 1929 and 1932, there were at least three plays put on the London stage suggesting that the war had been futile or worse, only one of them, *Journey's End*, by a man who had actually served in the trenches, R. C. Sherriff (Laurence Olivier made his debut in this play). The drama of the play is the relationship between Raleigh, a young man just out of school, and Stanhope, the commander of a platoon who was once at Raleigh's school. Stanhope has been rendered alcoholic as a consequence of his experiences in the war, which the puppyish Raleigh still regards as an adventure. In the last scene, Raleigh dies of wounds, comforted by Stanhope who until then has been merely irritated by his naivety. As Raleigh lies dead in the dugout, Stanhope leaves to attend to the continuing business of the war, and the audience is left with a melancholy apprehension of the waste and futility of the war, all the worse because of the fundamental nobility of the characters of which it has been able to take advantage.

The second play is by a man one would not normally associate with a cause as earnest as that of the re-remembering of the war, Noel Coward. His play *Post-Mortem* was produced in 1931. In this play, an officer killed in the trenches, John Cavan, returns thirteen years after his death to talk for a time to his friends and relations, to find out how they are now living. The title is clever, for not only is the main character dead, and all the action understood to take place after one of the greatest mass slaughters in history, but a post-mortem is the final court of appeal as to the illness of a patient. It allows you to find out what was really wrong with the patient.

John Cavan, being of the upper middle-class, discovers that life is going on without him and his fellow-dead; there is a lot of frivolity. His father, Sir James Cavan, is the proprietor of a tabloid newspaper, the *Daily Mercury*, that thrives on cheap patriotism of the kind that rejoices in war and sees a *casus belli* everywhere. In a scene of deep and effective if rather obvious satire, John attends a conference at his father's luxurious office at the newspaper, attended also by his secretary and lover, Miss Beaver, and his star writer, Alfred Borrow, who thinks and speaks in tabloid journalism stories. Borrow immediately begins to imagine how he is going to write up John's return from the dead:

BORROW: Return of Sir James Cavan's son after thirteen years! His mother, a white-haired Patrician lady smiled at our special representative with shining eyes. "My son," she said simply. Just that, but in those two words the meed of mother-love was welling over.

JOHN (*impersonally*): Worm, stinking little worm!

BORROW: A full page, nothing less than a full page. Have you any photographs of yourself aged two, then aged eight, then aged thirteen? Hurray for schooldays! Then seventeen, just enlisted, clear-eyed and clean-limbed, answering your country's call. "We're out to win," said Sir James Cavan's son, smilingly. Just that, but in those simple words what a wealth of feeling, what brimming enthusiasm.

Borrow continues in this vein, mixing up the war with the latest gossip and beauty hints, while John (a ghost) interjects "Filth—scavenging little rat!" and "I can't touch you with words or blows, the nightmare is too strong." The impression is given that the war was fought to make the world safe for tabloid journalism, that it was staged as part of the battle for circulation.

Then Lady Stagg-Mortimer joins the group. She, too, has lost a son in the war, but she appears to have recovered from it very well. As she enters, she declares what we are meant to suppose are her trivial moral, or moralistic, concerns:

LADY S-M[65]: How do you do? I should like a tongue sandwich, but no sherry. Sherry is the beginning of the end.

A little later she comments on Miss Beaver, the secretary:

---

65. I don't know whether, in those days, the initials S-M were popularly associated with sado-masochism. Certainly Coward was sly enough to smuggle them in.

LADY S-M: It's indecent! Merely intended to arouse the beast in men that's all she does it [showing too much neck] for. I know that kind, sly and quiet and utterly unreliable. . . . Look at the way she moves her hips when she walks!

Sir James invites his son to join a conference he is holding on the Great War:

SIR JAMES: You're fresh from the Great War.
BORROW: The Great War for Civilisation!
MISS BEAVER: The Great War for Freedom!
LADY S-M: The Great War for God!

By implication, of course, it was "really" the Great War for Nothing at All.

To illustrate just how unnaturally and with frivolous brutality patriotism makes people behave, Lady Stagg-Mortimer makes the following little speech:

LADY S-M: No one will ever know how we women of England suf-fered, suffered, suffered! We gave our loved ones, but proudly! We'd give them again—again—

By the end of the scene, John is so appalled by the shallowness, the incomprehension of the people who survived and prospered after the war was over, that—now hysterical—he says the following, foreshadowing General Millán-Astray's famous exclamation at Salamanca during the Spanish Civil War, *Viva la muerte!*:

JOHN: You didn't realise that all the sons that you gave, and the hus-bands you gave, and the lovers you gave in your silly pride were being set free. Free from your hates and loves and small pitiful prayers, for Eternity. You wouldn't have let them go so easily if you'd known, would you? You'll never find them again in your pantomime hell or your tinsel heaven. Long live War. Long live Death and Destruction and Despair!

The third play was *For Services Rendered* by Somerset Maugham, first published and performed in 1932, and the last play he ever wrote. During the Great War, Maugham had been a British government spy in St. Petersburg, an experience he used for his famous *Ashenden* stories; and although he was only too aware of the deficiencies of British culture, and chose to live whenever possible in France, he remained fundamentally patriotic—and at the beginning of the Second World War he even wrote a propaganda pamphlet (just as Coward was to write the patriotic *In Which We Serve*).

The play takes place in the home of Leonard Ardsley, the only lawyer in a small country town in England. Aged sixty-five, he is utterly conventional in his beliefs, in the end almost comically unable to understand the scale of the disasters that have befallen his family, largely as a result of the Great War.

One of his daughters, Ethel, has married unhappily beneath her, attracted to an unsuitable man by the uniform he wore, and has had to live with the consequences ever since. Another, Eva, remains unmarried in order to look after the son, Sydney, who was blinded in the war, and now spends his days at home, knitting or playing bridge and other games with specially adapted cards. Without knowing it or meaning to, Leonard Ardsley reveals symbolically how things can never be the same after the war, how historically and culturally an irreversible change has been wrought:

ARDSLEY: Poor old Sydney. It's been a great blow to me. I was hoping he would go into the business. He'd have been able to take a lot of the work off my hands now. I've paid for the war all right.

One of the characters in the play is called Stratton, a Navy man who is discharged in the cutbacks after the war with a small gratuity which he plunges into a garage in the small town and which, thanks to the Depression and his unbusinesslike ways, is near to bankruptcy. In order to stave it off, Stratton post-dates some cheques, for which he is about to be arrested, and commits suicide by shooting himself (off-stage). Unfortunately, Eva, who lost her fiancé in the war, taking years to overcome it, has fallen in unrequited love with him; he represents her last dream of escape from a life of looking after Sydney.

For most of the play, the blind Sydney remains sardonic, but towards the end he lets go with a bitter speech about the war that expresses to perfection the new orthodoxy about it:

SYDNEY: I know how dead keen we all were when the war started. Every sacrifice was worth it. We didn't say much about it because we were rather shy, but honour did mean something to us and patriotism wasn't just a word. And then, when it was all over, we did think that those of us who'd died hadn't died in vain, and those of us who were broken and shattered and knew they wouldn't be any more good in the world were buoyed up by the thought that if they'd given everything they'd given it in a great cause.

ARDSLEY: And they had.

SYDNEY: Do you still think that? I don't. I know that we were the dupes of the incompetent fools who ruled the nations. I knew that we were sacrificed to their vanity, their greed and their stupidity. And the worst of it is that as far as I can tell they haven't learned a thing. They're just as vain, they're just as greedy, they're just as stupid as they ever were. They muddle on, muddle on, and one of these days they'll muddle us all into another war. When that happens, I'll tell you what I'm going to do. I'm going out into the streets and cry, Look at me: don't be a lot of damned fools; it's all bunk what they're saying to you, about honour and patriotism and glory, bunk, bunk, bunk.

In the last scene, Eva has gone mad, refusing to accept that Stratton has killed himself and pretending that he is coming to the house to celebrate their engagement to be married. Ardsley has refused to notice or understand the intense emotion in his household, and remains absurdly complacent:

ARDSLEY: Well, I must say it's very nice to have a cup of tea by one's own fireside and surrounded by one's family. If you come to think of it we none of us have anything very much to worry

about . . . This old England of ours isn't done yet and I for one
believe in it and all it stands for.

Whereupon, Eva, mad, stands up and sings in a cracked voice:

God save our gracious King!
Long live our noble King!
God save our King!

and the curtain comes down.

The very title of the play could scarcely be more ironic than
it is: what follows, it says, is what you get for sacrificing yourself to patriotism. And the very success of this revaluation of the
meaning of the war—the normally jingoistic *Daily Mail* called it "a
magnificent play," and the very conservative *Daily Telegraph* called
it "a spiritual refreshment, and a sheer joy. . ."—must have made
it very difficult for politicians, had they felt so inclined, to face
up to Hitler by military means, even when the means needing to
be employed were minor. How could a population whose leading
lights had come to accept the evaluation of these three plays be
persuaded that, this time, war really was being waged to end war?
And so the re-evaluation of the war helped to make inevitable yet
another even larger and more terrible war.

If the re-evaluation of the war in the victor countries of Europe[66]
was as exemplified in these three plays, the works of men who
were by no means hotheads in any ideological sense, how could
the war be re-evaluated in the defeated countries? There was no
way of incorporating it into a memory that could be other than
humiliating to national self-esteem; and so the myth grew up that
the war was either a civil war of the Europeans bourgeoisie, the
kind of thing that is inevitable until the international proletarian
revolution renders national rivalry redundant and even inconceivable, or that the defeat was brought about by a stab in the back

---

66. In France, Gabriel Chevallier, the author of the humorous book *Clochemerle*, wrote a
bitter antiwar book, *La peur*. The influence everywhere of Remarque's book *All Quiet on the
Western Front* hardly needs mentioning.

at the behest of internal enemies and traitors. The latter view triumphed, with the results that we know all too well.

IF THAT'S WHAT THE VICTORS THOUGHT, WHAT ABOUT THE DEFEATED?

On the wall of my study is a print, drawn and signed by the great German artist George Grosz in the year of my mother's birth in Berlin. It is a street scene in that city, impoverished by the war; the buildings are rundown; the people on the street are a policeman, stolid and ready to commit any injustice; a worldly and knowing prostitute being eyed by a degenerate bourgeois with a cigar in one side of his mouth, his nose (as ever in Grosz's depictions of the degenerate bourgeois) mapped with spidery blood vessels; and a blind match-seller, obviously wounded in the war, now so down on his luck and nutrition that even his beard is skimpy and unhealthy.

It was to produce scenes like this that the war was fought and so many died. In the first act of *For Services Rendered*, Ethel offers Sydney her arm to walk out of the house, to which Sydney replies, "Spare a copper for a poor blind man, sir."

In Germany, disillusion bred a mad militarism; in Britain and France, a blind pacifism.

IO.

WHY ARE WE LIKE THIS (V)?

The Second World War destroyed European self-confidence once and for all. This was for two reasons that were synergistic in their effect: the first was the total loss of European power wrought by that war, and second was the nature of European behavior during it. No European power emerged with both its power intact and an historical record during the conflict that bear moral examination.

This immense cataclysm was not only caused by, but was also the cause of a deep intellectual, psychological, and spiritual crisis. If a nation with an immemorial history of cultural refinement and distinction in almost all fields of human endeavor could descend in a matter of a few years to industrialized barbarity, all on the basis of a theory that was so crude and vile that refutation would do it altogether too much honor, of what value was all the culture that went before? If extermination camp commandants could listen to Schubert lieder with tears in their eyes, of what value were Schubert lieder?[67] Worse still, were they not perhaps accomplices, or at least forerunners of the greatest crime in history?

NOTHING BUT-ISM REVISITED

This point of view, which is psychologically if not historiographically potent, was put forward in a book by an American historian, Daniel Goldhagen, entitled *Hitler's Willing Executioners*, published in 2000, which was a great success not only in English-speaking countries but also in Germany itself (where there was an insatiable thirst for guilt as a diploma of righteousness), and argued that the whole of German history was but a prelude to Hitler and the Final Solution. Nazism was the apotheosis, or the *telos*, of all German history hitherto; one could trace back the ideas and practices of Nazism through German history, and see that Nazism was always there, waiting to be born like a infant who is past his dates. One couldn't even listen to the B minor Mass any more without thinking of Julius Streicher. All Germans were tadpoles to Hitler's frog.[68]

From the purely rational point of view, this was preposterous. Of course, any historical phenomenon whatever must have both

---

67. Not long ago, I went to the house of a neighbor of mine, an antiquarian book dealer, to consult him over the problem of a binding of an eighteenth-century book in my possession. A great connoisseur of recordings, he was listening to what was obviously an old recording ("digitally remastered," as the saying goes) of a concert performance of the *Winterreise*. One heard the shuffling of the audience (coughs, scuffing of feet on the floor) in the background of what was a quite exquisite and sensitive performance. I asked my neighbor what the performance was. I forget now the singer, but he told me that it had been recorded in Berlin in 1943. 1943! The very year of Stalingrad and of the most ferocious implementation of the Final Solution. Perhaps one of the people in the audience making the background noise was Goebbels himself! This was not unlikely. I didn't know what to think, how to react. Could I abstract the performance altogether from the historical circumstances in which it was given? Was it psychologically possible, was it philosophically desirable, to do so? I said nothing to the dealer (whom I did not in the least suspect of Nazi sympathies— quite the reverse, he was the epitome of the decent Englishman) except a mild, "Oh, yes?" The fact that he could evidently listen to this performance, taking only its aesthetic qualities into consideration, confused me further. This incident occurred more than sixty years after the original performance. I am still not quite sure what to think.

68. I don't recall who it was who said that it was one of Austria's greatest achievements to have passed off Beethoven as an Austrian and Hitler as a German.

antecedents and causes. There must be a before and after, and events without causes belong to the realm of sub-atomic physics rather than to that of history. But history is lived forward, not backward, and foresight is rarely as comprehensive and accurate as hindsight.[69]

Consider, for example, my maternal grandfather, who was eventually forced to flee Germany and settled with his wife in China, where he (and she) died.[70] He was a doctor who had served as an officer in the German army during the First World War and was, I believe, a deep German patriot. Would he have been so if he had thought that all of German history was leading to the regime that forced him to flee the land of his birth and his affection, indeed was nothing but a prelude to it? Was he a stupid man who simply refused to see the writing on the wall? If so, he was far from unique; and an uncle of mine, who settled in England, and who was patriotic as far as England was concerned, remained nevertheless attached to the German culture in which had been raised. Were the words *Finis Austriae* that Sigmund Freud inscribed in his diary as the Nazi goons forced him into exile after the *Anschluss* words of triumph and relief, or were they words of melancholy? Were the words uttered by Thomas Mann when he arrived in America, having chosen exile from a Germany ruled by the Nazis, that "German culture is where I am," completely meaningless? Surely no one can think so.

However absurd in the abstract the historiography of Germany might be, which sees nothing in the past but a rehearsal or a foreshadowing of Nazism, it has a powerful effect. When Adorno said that, after Auschwitz, there could be no more poetry, everyone knew what he meant, though in the literal sense it was no more true than that after Auschwitz there could be no more *marrons glacés*. Not only could there be, but there were; perhaps more

---

69. In medicine, we call the tendency to be wise after the event "looking down the retrospectoscope."

70. Among the few things I ultimately inherited from him were the two Iron Crosses that he won in that war.

than ever, thanks to increasing prosperity. The same is not true of poetry, however.

The Nazis had shown us the abyss, but it was not a German abyss alone. It was a pan-European abyss. The Dutch, who hated the Germans for many years after the occupation, provided more men for the SS, *pro rata*, than any other nation. Many of the Flemish were enthusiastic Nazis, and the Walloon Léon Degrelle headed a pro-Nazi movement that sent volunteers to the eastern front. The behavior of the Slovaks, Croats, and Lithuanians hardly needs commentary. The Romanians behaved so brutally in Bessarabia and Transnistria that even some of the Germans felt moved to protest. There were limits, apparently, as to what was permissible even in the middle of a genocide. The Poles were hardly philosemites, and the Russians had little to learn from the Nazis in the matter of wholesale killing. The Russian government could have no objection to mass killing as such; for them it was merely a question of who was killing whom, and if the Nazis hadn't invaded the Soviet Union, the Nazis could have laid waste to the whole of Europe for all they cared, indeed they would rather have liked it. Spain kept out of the war, but it had arranged an internal massacre of its own, a million people being killed there between 1936 and 1940—equivalent perhaps to 12,000,000 in the United States today.

The Italians, it is true, were operetta monsters, though their fascism was scary enough. (I once attended a rally in Naples addressed by Alessandra Mussolini, in the castle there. The whole performance was absurd, preposterous, she most of all, looking like an advertisement for hair lacquer; nevertheless, to hear the full-throated roar of *Duce! Duce! Duce!* in an enclosed space was terrifying, and gave some indication of the intimidatory power of such movements. The men at the rally—there were no women—were mainly middle-aged or older, many of them with twisted bodies and above all faces, faces contorted, I surmised, by prolonged frustration. I went to laugh, and returned frightened.)

The Austrians claimed after the war to be the first victims of Nazism, though they provided many of the worst of the Nazis— including the Führer himself—and not only greeted the Anschluss with shining eyes but appropriated confiscated Jewish property with gusto. The Hungarians were equivocators; the Danes and Bulgarians preserved their honor. The Yugoslav partisans were far more concerned with destroying their rivals and establishing a communist dictatorship after the defeat of the Nazis (which they knew would be brought about by others) than with fighting the Germans. The Swiss were mercenary and lacking in scruple; the Irish divided—thousands joined up with the British forces, but a lot of nationalist sentiment was pro-Nazi, and De Valera famously signed the book of condolences at the German embassy on the death of Hitler, which was a quite unforced and therefore presumably a sincere action. Many of his social ideals, after all, were not so very far removed from those of the Nazis.

LAST AND BEST

Britain maintained its honor, no doubt, and its people displayed a sterling quality during the war; but what Churchill called its finest hour was really to be its final hour, and it was soon to experience profound historical doubts of its own as its empire dissolved, sometimes amicably and sometimes with acrimony, and was reassessed in the light of the new nationalist historiography.

VICHY IN THE BLOOD

I have so far left France out of this account, which (with the exception of Germany) most acutely had difficulties with memorialization and how to incorporate the war into its national history, difficulties whose effects are felt to this day. The preposterous Gaullist myth that everyone in France was a member of or sympathizer with the

Resistance or the Free French forces was designed to re-constitute national solidarity after what had, in effect, been a civil war as well as a foreign occupation.[71] Like all myths in tolerably free countries it was bound in the end to be questioned (though films such as *Le chagrin et la pitié* were prohibited from being screened in France for many years after the war, a procedure that was to be repeated after the Algerian war with Pontecorvo's *Battle of Algiers*; even a book detailing British assistance to the French Resistance, without which it could hardly have survived, was banned for publication in France until recently.)

Even until very recently, the wounds had been only weakly cicatrized. About five years ago, my French mother-in-law was going home on a bus to her flat in the 19th Arrondissement of Paris and fell to talking with a lady of her own age. This lady asked my mother-in-law where she lived, and she told her the address. "And which flat?" asked the lady. My mother-in-law told her, whereupon she burst into tears. By coincidence, my mother-in-law now lived in the very flat in which this lady, who was Jewish, had spent her war years hiding from the Germans (the building opposite, a local police station, had been the local komandatur during the Occupation), staying in the shadows and never daring to approach a window for fear of being seen. She had been taken in by a gentile family after her parents were deported, never to be seen again, with the co-operation of the French authorities: Does this story do credit or dishonor to France, indeed to human nature? That such bravery should have been necessary in the first place is horrible; that it existed admirable.

When I was visiting friends in a provincial town in South-West France shortly afterwards, the subject of the Resistance came up over lunch. The old lady who was present said something that would not all that long before have been almost unsayable in polite company: that she did not altogether admire the Resistance because, after the liberation, when she was a young woman,

71. "Remind me," says a character in Eugène Ionesco's play *Les chaises* (The Chairs) to a colonel, "in the last war, which side were you on? I forget." The play was first produced in 1953, and with the acuteness of genius summarizes in a few simple words the whole of the French, indeed the European, dilemma.

she had witnessed from her window some *résistants* shooting a neighbor dead in cold blood, though she knew for certain that he was not a collaborator. He was murdered, using the cover of the *épuration*, in pursuit of some purely private vengeance or rivalry. Historians have demonstrated pretty conclusively that this was not an isolated incident of such vengeance or rivalry.

Both stories would have required the witnesses to them to hold their silence for prolonged periods. On the one hand, French co-operation with the deportation of about 70,000 Jews from France,[72] very few of whom returned, was for years a taboo subject, though the lady on the bus must have known all about it, as of course did many others; on the other hand, so was the less than immaculate history of the Resistance after the war, such that the old lady in the second story could not have revealed what she had seen with her own eyes, or draw any conclusion from it.

Here are just a few of the questions that the occupation of France raised and, in fact, still raises.

Was Pétain a legitimate ruler, indeed the duly constituted legal heir of the Third Republic?

Was he motivated by the desire to save what he could in the direst circumstances, and was he right to try to do so? (Even de Gaulle sometimes admitted that, after the defeat, France needed two strings to its bow.)

What was, and what should have been, the attitude of the French population to the Occupation and to Pétain's government? Was the widespread denunciation of others to the police during the Occupation a sign of French support for Nazism,[73] or was it

---

72. If in 1900 you had been told that within the next half century a major European power would carry out a genocide against the Jews, and been asked to guess which it would be, you would almost certainly have placed Russia first, but been unable to decide between France and Germany for second place. Drumont's book *La France juive* went through scores of editions and probably sold more copies than books by German or Austrian anti-semites. This, it seems to me, is another refutation of Goldhagen's thesis.

73. For the unedifying history of informing during the occupation, see *La délation sous l'Occupation*, André Halimi. Robert Gellateley, in *The Gestapo and German Society*, showed that informing in Nazi Germany was not merely a duty imposed by a totalitarian state, but a pleasure for quite a lot of the population. The British should not be too complacent, however. Not only can people who shop tax evaders expect a financial reward, but from time to time the government, under the pretense that it is the careful guardian of the

merely a temporary disinhibition of the common human desire to do harm to one's neighbor? Can one demand of people that they be heroes, or merely that they do not do anything too bad?

What was the status, *vis-à-vis* the desire for freedom, of the Resistance, given that a fairly large proportion of it was made up of communists, who themselves were the most ferocious enemies of intellectual liberty even within their ranks, let alone outside their ranks, who themselves ran an extensive system of surreptitious denunciation backed up by unscrupulous spying,[74] who had supported the Molotov-Ribbentrop pact and who ever afterwards proved themselves to be utterly blind to, if not outright supportive of, some of the worst political oppression and mass-killing in history?

Of course, similar unanswered and perhaps unanswerable questions could, *a fortiori*, be asked of the Germans. What exactly was the level of support of the population for the Nazis, and because of what policies? What did the population know, or what could it have known if it had wished to know? Did Hitler remain popular to almost the end because he was able to bribe the German people with the spoils of other nations and the products of their slave labor, as Gotz Ally alleges?

AFTER LIBERATION, MASSACRE

In the case of France, the historical record was contorted by the colonial wars on which it was embroiled soon after the liberation. Indeed, on the very day of the German surrender, the French army committed a massacre of Algerian nationalist demonstrators in

---

public moneys, runs an advertising campaign asking the public to inform on those who defraud the social security system by working surreptitiously while claiming benefits. All denunciations, say the campaigns, will be dealt with confidentially. I remember the advertisement for one such campaign with a picture of a sewer rat and the legend "Rat on a rat!" What the advertisement did not make clear was whether the picture represented the person who ratted, the person ratted upon, or both.

74. See, for example, *La chasse aux traîtres du PCF*, Michel Dreyfus.

Setif. No one knows exactly how many people died—officially 2,000, though the nationalists claimed (and claim) for purposes just as dishonest that 100,000 died in the few surrounding days. Whatever the true figure, the events were hushed up and everything done to forget them; but the nationalists did not forget, and they started the war that led seven years later to Algerian independence (in between the massacre and the outbreak of the war, the French put down a nationalist rebellion in Madagascar in which up to 100,000 are estimated to have been killed). As the world knows, this war was carried out with brutality on both sides but, as is always the case, the army of the government killed more than the rebels fighting for power. The defenders of the status quo always kill more people in general, including noncombatants— but this fact, in turn, is so well-known that revolutionists take advantage of it to drum up sympathy for themselves.

The history of the French occupation of Algeria a very contorted one, and to this day arouses strong emotions in France. The story of the status and fate of the Algerian Jews illustrates the difficulties that a post-imperial state inevitably has with its own history.

When the French first tried to invade Algeria in the sixteenth century, the Algerian Jews sided with the Moslem power, perhaps partly from a consideration of who was more likely to win, but also because they believed that they would be treated better by the Moslem than the Christian power. This is not to say there was a golden age of tolerance and equality in sixteenth-century Algeria; Islam has as yet no theory of religious equality under the law (which is one of the reasons why it has such difficulty with modernity); all that was necessary for the Jews to side with the Moslems was that they could choose the lesser evil.

De facto tolerance, such as usually develops when people live side by side for a long time, was punctuated by pogroms and massacres, and by the time the French arrived in Algeria in 1831, the position of the Jews was (according to contemporary accounts) an unenviable one. There were sumptuary laws against them, they had to wear a yellow badge, they had to acknowledge their inferiority in their dealings with Moslems in the most humiliating ways. The French occupation came as liberation to them.

One of the first legal measures of the new Third Republic was to pass the *Decret Crémieux*, a measure first mooted under Napoleon, giving all the Jews of Algeria French citizenship. At first sight, this might seem like a liberal and generous thing to have done, but it had its ironies: It stoked up resentments and contributed ultimately to the end of the two-thousand-year presence of Jews in the country.

No one likes to go from being master of the house to third-class citizen, from oppressing others to being oppressed oneself. The Moslems, who had immemorially been the superiors of the Jews, now became their social inferiors. Not surprisingly, the Jews began to adopt European ways, and in the process to become successful, though most remained what they had always been, that is to say poor.

Unfortunately, their social ascension was not altogether appreciated by those who had granted them the opportunity. Drumont, for example, was a *député* to the national Assembly for Algiers, and the French colonial press was viciously anti-semitic. The impoverished *pieds noirs*, half of whom came from Spain and Italy and were themselves not certain of their status as Frenchmen, were resentful that such favoritism, as they saw it, should have been shown to their competitors, a half-oriental race whom even the despised Arabs despised. Indeed, the anti-semitic riots of the late 1890s were conducted not by the Arabs, but by the French, or at any rate European, settlers.

The Jews of Algeria became more and more westernized. In photographs of them taken in the first years of the twentieth century, half of them were still dressed in the Turkish style, and only half in western (some, it is true, managed to combine for a time elements of the two); by the 1930s, they were so comprehensively westernized that they wore western clothes as if it were inconceivable that they should wear any other. This did not please the Moslem Algerians who, always with a theological justification ready to dislike the Jews, thought they had gone over entirely to the enemy. In 1934, there were anti-Jewish riots in Constantine, which the authorities were suspiciously slow to put down. No doubt infused themselves with anti-semitic feelings, they were also cautious about being too eager to side with Jews against Moslems, since nationalist feeling had already begun to develop.

Then came the Armistice, and the French authorities of Algeria went over to Pétain rather than to de Gaulle. Within short order, the Jews of Algeria were third-class citizens again, of less account in the authorities' eyes than the Moslem Algerians. It was a terrible time for the Algerian Jews, subject to every kind of oppression; with the liberation came the restoration of the French citizenship, though somewhat tardily.

When the Algerian war broke out they were caught squarely in the middle. Despite their treatment at the hands of the French state, they were attached to the "republican values" of France; and yet, they could hardly fail to understand the nationalists' point of view. Neutrality is impossible in a war like the Algerian, however; and though the nationalists, who after all were secularists with socialist leanings, promised them complete equality in the new Algeria, they understood secularism's shallow roots in a society such as Algeria's, and when independence came they emigrated en masse to France. Two millennia of history, by no means all happy, came to an end.

It is rather difficult to construct out of this story a straightforward account of France as the French often prefer to see it, that is to say the land *par excellence* of liberty, equality, and fraternity, qualities that, as the universalist nation, they like to think they gave to the world, but none of the three of which was always much in evidence in French-ruled Algeria. And indeed, with the Algerian War of Independence came further difficulties.

It was twenty years before the word "war" was used officially of the war. Until then, the war had been merely "events" and "a police action to restore order." In 1958, the French journalist Henri Alleg, a member of the communist party, who had edited a daily newspaper in Algeria sympathetic to the nationalists, published an account in France, *La question*, of his torture by French forces after his arrest for having given aid and comfort to the enemy. The book (whose title was a clever play on words, implying not only the question of French sovereignty in Algeria, but recalling the use of the word in pre-revolutionary French jurisprudence, when putting the question meant the torture of suspects) was banned, but only after 60,000 copies had been sold. Reference to it in newspapers was forbidden. Sartre wrote an introduction to the book in which he said, "For most Europeans in Algeria, the colonials have divine right, and the natives are sub-human;" he also wrote a long essay on the book which, like other commentary on the book, was banned.

What Alleg had written was true, of course. From then on, there could be no real doubt about the methods used by the French to retain control of Algeria. A prominent French journalist of more conservative views wrote that the French had lost the right to reproach the Germans for the massacre at Oradour, the village in France in which all 642 inhabitants were killed by the SS in "retaliation" for increasing Resistance activity.[75]

After Algeria obtained its independence, there was an almost complete silence in France, a wilful forgetting, of what had happened.[76] There were no memorials to commemorate the dead (the comparative absence of memorialization of the Second World War, from which France nominally emerged as a victor, but with 600,000 dead, when every village has a prominent war memorial dedicated to the First World War, is surely significant).

At the beginning of the twenty-first century, two shockwaves passed over France, at least in its intellectual life, again because of the Algerian war. The first was caused by the "revelation" that the Harkis, the Algerians who had aided or fought for France

---

75. The general commanding the SS Division responsible for the massacre, Heinz Lammerding, went on to a successful business career at the height of the *Witschaftswunder*. Of the twenty-one people tried in France in 1953 for the massacre, fourteen were French citizens of Alsatian origin. They claimed that they were inducted into the SS *malgré nous*, in spite of ourselves, and in effect that they were only obeying orders. Nevertheless, they were found guilty; but an outcry in Alsace, where there was some agitation for autonomy from France, led to their release. This in turn led to an outcry in the region of Oradour.

76. In marked contrast to Algeria, of course, with its constant official reference to the war of independence, passing over in its entirety the fact that the first fruit of independence was a massacre of perhaps 60,000 Algerians who had supported the French, and the installation of a kleptocratic regime that eventually provoked a reaction leading to a brutal civil war, a regime that never for an instant allowed freedom of opinion: suggesting that the war of independence was not and had never been a freedom struggle, but a power struggle.

during the war of independence, a hundred thousand of whom had escaped to France before they could be massacred by their Algerian brothers, had been very badly treated since their arrival in the land of the Declaration of the Rights of Man. Far from being greeted as worthy and indeed meritorious *enfants de la patrie*, they were dumped in camps out of sight and out of mind, where they remained for up to thirty years. Their fate was better than it would have been had they remained in Algeria, of course, but nevertheless they had been treated shamefully. It could hardly have been the case than no one knew of their fate in France until then—the very excuse that the Germans, after all, had used about the concentration camps in their midst—but the sudden crisis of conscience, complete with books published at the same time and endless newspaper coverage, was briefly disturbing but without obvious practical effect. The shameful secret was buried again almost at once, though it is a fair bet that it will emerge again conveniently when anyone wants to call into question France's democratic and liberal credentials.

The second shock wave was caused by the affair of General Paul Aussaresses, which revealed the multiple and almost unassimilable ironies of French history. Aussaresses, a career officer, joined up straight away with the Free French: there was therefore no taint of Vichy about him. But he then went on to fight for the suppression of Indochinese and Algerian independence, and in 2001 he published a memoir in which he not only admitted the torture that had been used in Algeria (which was hardly deniable, though the fact shocked some people in France as if Henri Alleg had never written his book), but also claimed that it had been entirely justified, and indeed that it had been sanctioned by the highest authorities, not least of whom was the former, supposedly left-wing, President of the Republic, François Mitterrand.

There was a great outcry, with calls for Aussaresses to be tried for crimes against humanity. He was stripped of his *Légion d'honneur*, but he, not without justification, decried the decision as hypocritical. Mitterrand, after all, had supported the war in Algeria at the time; it is vanishingly unlikely that he did not know the methods used during it.

Moreover, Mitterrand, by then dead, was a very shadowy figure indeed. He started out on the far right of French politics, was an important official under Vichy, for which services he received a high decoration from Pétain, then he went over to the Resistance, and finally to the left. Whether these changes corresponded to anything in the nature of actual convictions can now never be known; suffice it to say that Mitterrand, shortly after his elevation to the presidency, invited René Bousquet to the Elysée.

UNEQUAL TREATMENT

Now Bousquet was, like Aussaresses, a man who had had his *Légion d'honneur* (awarded for meritorious services during the floods that affected South-West France in 1930) removed from him. In his case, the decoration was removed because he had been so prominent a collaborator. It was restored to him in 1957.

He had been a police chief during the Occupation and had arranged for the deportation of Jews from Paris and elsewhere, certainly to their deaths, and had personally gone beyond even what the Germans had required of him. Moreover, he had also participated in the destruction of a part of the old port of Marseille, leading to the deportation of 2,000 residents, because the Germans considered it a "nest of terrorists." It is probable, however, that at the end of his police career, he was playing a double game, protecting and even encouraging the Resistance.

He suffered the minimum punishment possible for his crimes after the liberation (unlike, say, Robert Brasillach, the gifted writer who supported the Germans but never actually killed anyone, who was shot). He then made money, and was a financial backer of the left wing in France, including, it is believed, of Pierre Mendès-France, the Jewish Prime Minister. The deporter of Jews became the financial backer of a prominent Jewish politician!

Eventually, not for reasons of principle one suspects, Mitterrand cut off relations with Bousquet, who, as evidence (which, of course, had always been available) mounted against him, was sent for trial: fortunately he was shot dead just before his trial, in the course of which he would no doubt have spilled many beans in an attempt to demonstrate that he was not guiltier, and no worse morally, than many others he could name.

To return briefly to the Algerian question. In reaction to the view that the history of the French colonization of Algeria was nothing but rapine and oppression, a law was passed in the National Assembly in 2005 requiring schools to teach that the French presence in North Africa and other colonies had its positive and constructive side. At one time, this would hardly have outraged Karl Marx, since he was a great believer in the positive effects of colonialism, at least at the right time. For Marxists, it would be completely undialectical, at least in theory, to say that European colonialism had been completely destructive in its effects. On the contrary, it had precisely the positive effects—bringing economic, technological, and intellectual advancement—that the law demanded that history teachers in school recognize and pass on to their pupils.

But there were several objections to the law, practical and theoretical. To many people, it sounded like apologetics for colonialism, a bit like justifying Hitler on the grounds of the *Autobahnen* or Mussolini on the grounds of the punctuality of trains. Since the end of the Algerian war, moreover, there had developed in France a population of perhaps 5,000,000 people of North African descent, who might find the law offensive; and since they were already predominantly located in *les zones sensibles*, the sensitive areas, of cities (as the euphemism for suburban ghettoes puts it), the law was deemed to be an unnecessary irritant—though it is likely that those who objected to it would not object to the teaching of the historiography of French colonialism as the history of rapine and massacre, and of the coming to power of the Algerian dictatorship as an unequivocal "liberation"), with it consequent effect on national morale.[77]

77. In a very impressive speech of acceptance of an honorary degree at Oxford, the current Prime Minister of India, Manmohan Singh, enumerated the negative and positive effects of British rule in India. But then, of course, India is one of the few examples of decolonization in the twentieth century that led to an increase in freedom rather than to a despotism of a different, and often worse, kind.

WE HAVE NO HISTORY

In the event, President Chirac used his powers to suppress the law, saying that "In the Republic, there is no official history. It is not for the law to write history. Writing history is for historian." Splendid as this no doubt is, it is not entirely honest. Not only has the French legislature passed laws prohibiting the denial of the Holocaust and the Armenian genocide, but what is Bastille Day if not an implicit version of history, one that is just as contestable as that of colonialism, if about events a little (but not much) longer ago? Zhou En-lai famously replied, when asked what he thought of the effects of the French Revolution were, "It is too early to tell"; the meaning of the French Revolution is still uncertain, and recently a large book was published in France, *Le livre noir de la Révolution française* (a counterpart to the Black Book of Communism) in which much was made of the terrible massacres in the Vendée, which establish that the Revolution was no more a manifestation of the will of the whole French people than was the Resistance.

President Chirac's involvement in these matters was a great deal more honorable and straightforward that his predecessor's. Unfortunately, he is regarded by most of his countrymen as having been a crook in the more ordinary sense of the term.

Finally, to complete the picture—or rather to turn it into a canvas by Jackson Pollock—let me just point out that Henri Alleg (to say nothing of Sartre) was as deep-dyed a hypocrite as it is possible for anyone to be. A follower of Stalin, he believed strongly in the justification of mass-murder, terrorization of whole populations, deliberately induced famines, and the total suppression of all intellectual freedom, to say nothing of absurd cults of personality. He cannot hide behind the veil of alleged ignorance, for to do so is to commit precisely the same crime that he accuses apologists for French colonial policy in Algeria of having done. If he did not know, his ignorance was wilful; therefore, he knew, and therefore it is reasonable to infer that he approved of all the terrible things done in the name of his chosen ideal. He is like the Peronist who, when asked what he thought of torture, replied that it depended on who was being tortured and who was doing the torturing.

Truly, here is *"un passé qui ne passe pas,"* a past that is never over, never done with.

II.

WHY ARE WE LIKE
THIS (VI)?

I have dwelt a little on France, but I do not mean to imply that
the problems of history are unique to it: far from it. The case of
Germany hardly needs comment. Almost every country in Europe
suffers from similar problems, if not always quite so acutely.

Belgium, for example, has not only its collaborationist history
during the war, but its Congo, a history that it too tried to forget
but which the presence of so many Congolese in the country now
brings back to mind, at least subliminally. Conrad's *Heart of Dark-
ness* was scarcely an exaggeration of the horrors of King Leopold's
rule; and the fact is that a history of horrors insufficiently acknowledged or incorporated into the national psyche has a tendency to
return like Banquo's ghost and ruin proceedings.

I have already alluded to Dutch participation in the war, but
there is the fact that almost the first concern of the newly liberated Dutch from the Nazi yoke was to suppress the movement for
national independence in the East Indies, which led to an unsuc-

cessful war that cost 100,000 lives.[78] Even the pacifist Dutch have a violent skeleton in their cupboard.

The Spanish, of course, have their *leyenda negra*, black legend, to contend with: that is to say, the idea that Spanish colonialism was a catalogue of horrors and nothing but horrors, including every conceivable cruelty, abuse, and act of genocide, a legend that has recently (with the 500th anniversary of Columbus's voyage) taken on new life, demographic studies showing that populations declined by 90 percent in the first hundred years after the Spanish arrived. The *leyenda negra* was originated in other Western European powers who were dissatisfied with Spain's American hegemony and seized upon the writings of Fray Bartolome de las Casas for propaganda purposes; the use to which the legend is now put is to discredit European civilization as a whole.

Meanwhile, Spain is digging up (quite literally) its recent past in fossae of thousands of people murdered during and after the Civil War. Roughly speaking, nothing much happened in or to Spain between the destruction of the Indians and the Civil War, unless you count its invention of the concentration camp in Cuba.

Italy's thirst for great power status led it to an adventure in what is now Libya, wresting the country from Turkish sovereignty, and in the process killing 100,000 of a very small population. Having lost the Battle of Adowa in 1896 when an Italian force was beaten by the Abyssinians, Mussolini took revenge by, among other things, the use of poison gas from airplanes. And that is without considering the domestic crimes of Mussolini.

British colonization was far from benign. Although the history of the British in Ireland has a good many more ambiguities, especially in its later period, than nationalist historiography would until recently admit, no one would consider it a cause of national pride, to say the very least. Why the British thought they had the right, and sometimes even the duty, to claim the sovereignty of large tracts of other people's land is something that escapes me; I don't give you permission to appropriate my house, even if I think

---

78. Soekarno, of course, was vehemently opposed to anyone's liberty but his own.

you would decorate it in better taste than I, and indeed had more money to spend in it.

The British used concentration camps against the Boers, and poisoned gas in Iraq. Although in general they decolonized less unwillingly than the French, and certainly than the Portuguese, there was some violence, for example in Aden and Cyprus, and most notably in Kenya. Again, the meaning (if events can be said to have a meaning) of the Mau-Mau rebellion might be ambiguous, in that it was primitive, without clearly articulated aims, and confined mainly to the Kikuyu; certainly the newly independent Kenyan state was not keen to memorialize it in the way, for example, that the Algerian War of Independence was memorialized in Algeria for purposes of legitimating in perpetuity the new regime. But what is important, from the point of view of constructing a certain kind of history, is that many thousands died in the suppression of the revolt, and that much brutality was used in it.

Then there is the Atlantic slave trade, in which Britain played so large a role, with millions transported across the ocean in the most terrible conditions. The fact that it could be carried on only with African assistance does not alter Britain's guilt; as for Britain's preponderant role in abolishing the same slave trade, that is easily explicable, or explicable away (which for these purposes is the same thing) by a change in national self-interest.

There is the genocide of the Tasmanian aborigines, shortly after the British took possession of Australia. It does not matter that there was no genocide, and that, though the Tasmanian aborigines did die out, it was not genocide that killed them. The genocide has now entered the roll-call of genocides through history; what counts is not what happened but what is thought to have happened.

The Bengal famine in 1943 in India, only four years before the end of British rule, was one of the worst of many famines during that rule. Since Amartya Sen's demonstration that famines only occur where there is no democracy or political freedom, the famine can be represented as Britain's fault entirely. Another one or two million people died during Partition, and though this cannot be attributed simply and solely to British misdeeds, it happened under British sovereignty. Life expectancy in India rose dramatically after independence, and while this might in large part be attributed to technical advance, it can hardly be said to redound to Britain's credit.

In short, it is not difficult to construct a history of most European countries that is nothing but that of crime and folly, leaving out the achievement altogether.

12.

WHY ARE WE LIKE THIS (VII)?

Why should anyone wish to construct a national history that is nothing but crime and folly?

I think there are three main reasons. The first is bitterness at the loss of European power and significance in the world at the end of the Second World War. While it is relatively easy to incorporate the less glorious aspects of a national history while the country concerned remains either powerful or still struggling for national existence against others, it is much harder to do so once that power has been lost or that struggle has passed: for it is then more difficult to explain away or diminish those less glorious aspects by reference to higher purpose or greater glory. If your nation has made an omelette, you can forgive it for also having broken eggs; but if it has broken eggs and there is no longer an omelette to show for it, disillusion and even disgust set in.

ANOTHER WAY OF BEING IMPORTANT

Second, limitless guilt being a form of grandiosity, the past commission of great crimes is a consolation for those who have lost power. It assures them that, notwithstanding their loss of the more immediate trappings of power, important, indeed determining, factors in the current situation of the world are traceable to them. If Africa is an abominable mess, it is because of what we, the former colonizing nations, did to it: ergo, we are still important. Of course, this does have the somewhat unfortunate consequence that we regard Africans as so powerless that they are incapable even of making their own mess, or of contributing very much to it; but it is better, at least for the *amour propre*, to be responsible for a lot of harm, indeed great evil, than for not very much. That is why we can go almost seamlessly from believing that everything we have done and do is the best, that we are civilizing the world, to the belief that we have ruined the world and that everything that is bad in it is ultimately traceable to us.

Third, a miserabilist history is a very useful instrument in securing if not a social revolution, then at least a change or expansion of elites. If the past of a country is nothing but a record of crime and folly, it is clear that it must have been led by quite the wrong people. This is a very important thought in countries in which the numbers of educated people are increasing very fast: people who believe that they have a right, by virtue of their education, to a more than average voice in the running of the country.[79] Bureaucracies must be created to right the wrongs of the past, the very bureaucracies that absorb the newly educated thousands and millions. Miserabilism thus combines business with pleasure.

In Britain at least, the scions of the ruling class, embittered by the fact that the cup of power had been dashed from their lips in

---

79. Joe Keller says, in Arthur Miller's *All My Sons*, "Everybody's gettin' so Goddam educated in this country there'll be nobody to take away the garbage. . . . It's a tragedy: you stand on the street today and spit, you're gonna to hit a college man." Of course, there are always Third World immigrants to take away the garbage, but their children are not content to remain garbage collectors, nor should they be.

the last few decades, turned with fury on the culture that had similarly raised them to be a ruling class and so disappointed them with the small scale of their power; and so a combination of satire and miserabilism took hold, destroying utterly all national confidence. Not only was the country worth nothing now, but it had never been worth anything.

There is, of course, plenty of grist to the European miserabilist mill, as there had been for the whole of humanity ever since the Loss of Eden. But I don't see how anyone can walk around Paris, say, or Venice, or Rome, or indeed anywhere (when rightly considered) and see only crime and folly, and no achievement, almost all of it that of European civilization. Instead, we have all taken to heart Mahatma Gandhi's famous quip when he was in London and asked what he thought of western civilization, that he thought it would be a good idea.

13.

THE CONSEQUENCES

Most Europeans are not religious. Most Europeans do not believe in any large political project, whether it be that of a social class, the nation, or of Europe as a whole. Most Europeans have no concept any longer of *la gloire*, that easily derided notion that can nevertheless impel people to the highest endeavor, and to transcend themselves and their most immediate interests. Most Europeans would now mock the very idea of a European civilization and therefore cannot feel much inclination to contribute to it.[80]

Miserabilism leads to a mixture of indifference towards the past and hatred of it.[81] This hatred is visible in the architecture and

---

80. When I was a child of about ten or eleven, my teacher took me to the National Portrait Gallery in London. I was very deeply impressed, so deeply in fact that I formed the childish ambition to do something that made me worthy one day to take my place on its walls. Would any child form such an ambition today? Would any teacher not be horrified that his pupil had formed so patriotic an ambition?

81. Ignorance of the past is not incompatible with certainty, indeed absolute conviction, that it was terrible and nothing but terrible. School children are often now often taught about the slave trade and the Holocaust, but which came before which evades them. I met

urban planning of Europe since the war. The Franco-Swiss monster Le Corbusier, whose main talent by far was for self-promotion, is still a hero to French architects, and he wanted to pull down the whole of Paris in order to turn it into a French reinforced concrete Novosibirsk. (The epidemiology of graffiti in European cities should be enough to persuade anyone of the social effects of Corbusier's favorite material, reinforced concrete.) This destruction is what French architects, probably, dream of doing. But to what kind of mind could such a thought even occur for an instant? As it turns out, to quite a few such minds. The much praised French architect Jean Nouvel, who (to the eternal shame of the United States) won a Pritzker Prize, cannot wait to destroy Paris once and for all by building glass and concrete towers in it everywhere, on the grounds that Paris cannot remain "a museum."[82] Of course, Nouvel has already managed that most difficult of all architectural feats, the production of a museum in Paris even uglier than the *Centre Pompidou,* that is to say the new and gimcrack, though no doubt very expensive, *Musée du quai Branly.* Not coincidentally, one feels, he presents himself in photographs for the press as a thug, ugly, shaven-headed, and dressed all in black. Of course, he is far worse than a mere thug, since his activities affect millions.

THE CONSTRUCTIVE URGE IS ALSO DESTRUCTIVE

This mania for destruction was by no means confined to France. The Dutch politician (who became Prime Minister) Joop den Uyl wanted to pull down quite a lot of seventeenth-century Amsterdam, surely some of the greatest and most elegant domestic architecture in the history of the world, in order to build a highway to the station and "socially just" housing projects of the kind that may now be seen the world over.

---

many young people in the course of my medical practice in England to whom the words "Ten sixty-six" were more likely to conjure up a price than a date.

82. Even now, it remains one of the richest and most economically productive and efficient cities in the world.

The city council of Bath wanted, in the 1950s, to pull down the entire Georgian city—again one of the greatest triumphs of urban design in the whole world—and replace it with architecture in what might be called the dysfunctional functionalist style. Protest prevented it from doing so just in time; but the very thought that it could have occurred to anyone to pull down Bath is enough to induce a profound despair.

More recently, the council of the elegant Regency town of Cheltenham in England decreed that any new building should be out of keeping with its Regency heritage: pastiche being for it a far worse crime than the total annihilation of a visual horizon, in so far as the former implies an inability of current architects and urban planners to improve upon their predecessors—by precisely people responsible for a history of nothing but crime and folly.

This mania for destruction, often carried out in lesser degrees by the strategic placement of a terrible building that the eye cannot escape (the *Tour Montparnasse* in Paris is a particularly fine example of the genre), is a symptom of an impotent rage that Europe has been left behind, is not longer in the vanguard of anything. It is also a kind of magical thinking: that by adopting the externals of modernity somehow modernity itself will be achieved and mastered. In Nigeria, there are buildings that are called by their developers and owners "The Ultra-Modern Building Complex," that are completely inappropriate to the conditions obtaining in the country; power cuts mean that you have to walk up tens of flights of stairs in the stifling heat, and the supposed air-conditioning system means that the windows cannot be opened, with the result that mold creeps everywhere. The old colonial buildings, with the natural air-conditioning provided by shaded verandas, were vastly better and more functional, but they were not ultra-modern, and are therefore despised, as well as being symbols of a past that at least the elite of the country despised and hated.

You are not called upon to defend what does not really exist for you, or that you think is not of worth. Of course, too strong a sense of having inherited what is worth preserving can induce a paranoid defensiveness, and incline you to see enemies everywhere; but too weak a sense inclines you to see enemies nowhere. Nor can you even rise to challenges posed perfectly honorably by competitors. And because of their history, or rather their obsession with the worst aspects of that history, Europeans do not even feel able any more to admit that they wish to preserve their own way of life, for fear of historical atavism. When I delight in some corner of England or France that appears to me to have preserved the old national characteristics, I fear to express my delight, because I shall be accounted a xenophobe. Like "Forestry with Pride," an attachment to his culture is, for the European, the beginning of the slippery slope.

HEDONISM AT BEST, COMFORT AT WORST

What is left for Europeans? This present life being all that counts, indeed all that truly exists, it remains for them to seek the good life, the enjoyable and comfortable life, the abundant life, for themselves and themselves alone. They mistrust grander projects: for has history not sufficiently demonstrated that that way madness lies? After the end of the Second World War, the Germans put all their formidable intelligence, industriousness, and organizational ability that they had previously employed in the search for world conquest and on the commission of genocide into creating both the workshop of the world and a social-democratic state in which the citizens would feel and be forever secure. There seemed nothing in between the two: it was total war or total peace.

What was true of Germany was true of the rest of Europe. What counted from now on was the standard of living and the means by which it could be protected from the vicissitudes of economic life. Europeans are fearful of the future because they fear the past; they are desperate to hang on to what they have already got, what the French call *les acquis*, because it represents for them the whole purpose of their existence. They do this even when the situation calls for flexibility, and when a lack of flexibility threatens the entire system. Of course, the cost to everyone of the generous social security provisions is great and abuses are common; but it is a price that Europeans are willing to pay because security and stability (even if they ultimately prove illusory) are worth so much to them.

So important is the standard of living to them that they see children not as the inheritors of what they themselves inherited, as essential to the meaning of life, but as obstructions to the enjoyment of life, as a drain on resources, an obstacle to next year's holiday in Bali or wherever it might be, a commitment that forecloses on certain possibilities, a hurdle in the way of the exercise of choice. No doubt children are so much of a hurdle because everyone has to pay so much for the social security that is his guarantee against an abrupt lowering of standard of living; and this also means that if those holidays in Bali are going to be paid for, the potential mothers have to go out to work as well as the potential fathers, with little time for child-bearing and raising. If all this means that life will not continue after them, at least not in the same way, and if it means that Italy (for example) becomes before long an Albano-Somali peninsula, so be it, there was never anything worth preserving anyway, if history is understood correctly; and if a man enjoys his life, and life is for enjoyment, what more is there to be said? A man who has enjoyed his life, who has gone to Bali on holiday many times, has not wasted it.

Dean Acheson once said that Britain had lost an empire and not found a role. You might say of Europe that it had lost its purpose, and not found any to replace it.

AMERICAN ENVOI

The great upheavals which precede changes of civilizations such as the fall of the Roman Empire and the foundation of the Arabian Empire, seem at first sight determined more especially by political transformations, foreign invasion, or the overthrow of dynasties. But a more attentive study of these events shows that behind their apparent causes the real cause is generally seen to be a profound modification in the ideas of the peoples. The true historical upheavals are not those which astonish us by their grandeur and

> violence. The only important changes whence the renewal
> of civilizations results, affect ideas, conceptions, and beliefs.
> The memorable events of history are the visible effects of
> the invisible changes of human thought. The reason these
> great events are so rare is that there is nothing so stable in a
> race as the inherited groundwork of its thoughts.
>
> GUSTAVE LE BON, *THE CROWD*

It is vain in human affairs to search for final causes: changes in ideas, conceptions, and beliefs, of the kind Le Bon made responsible for upheavals, are themselves historically caused as much as other events. In other words, events and ideas are in eternal dialogue. Events affect men's ideas; men's ideas affect events. The desire for a final explanation of everything is a manifestation of impatience, intolerance of uncertainty, and an understandable, if lazy, wish for a nice, quiet state of mind in which everything has been settled in advance once and for all, and thought is therefore no longer necessary.

We have, however, often to act as if we did know the final causes of things, at least sufficiently well to take reasonable action. Antibiotics were used effectively before anyone had any idea of the way in which they worked biochemically. We generally have to act as if we already knew enough, though it is advisable to keep in mind that often we do not.

Is there anything in the European experience from which Americans might learn? Americans are apt to believe in American exceptionalism, for a number of reasons.[83] First, of course, America is situated on a continent that has been isolated geographically from conflicts in Asia and Europe, and has never faced any serious threat from its neighbors or near-neighbors. It still faces no such threats, whereas Western Europe has Russia always

---

83. "If we have to use force, it is because we are America. We are the indispensable nation. We stand tall. We see further into the future." It would take a book in itself to disentangle the folly, hubris, and evil contained in Madeleine Albright's famous, or infamous, words. To begin with, the notion of the indispensable nation implies that all the others are dispensable. One might have hoped that we had stopped thinking of millions of people, or even of one person, in terms of dispensability. Never in the field of human history has a woman learnt so little from so much as Madeleine Albright.

on the doorstep, a country that for hundreds of years has placed the military strength of the state far ahead of all considerations of the welfare of the population.

Then the United States is a nation founded on a coherent and attractive, if not necessarily the most profound, philosophy, unlike all other nations that, as it were, "just growed." The philosophy upon which the United States is founded is an optimistic philosophy, one that suggests boundless possibilities. In an age of mass migration, at least in one direction, this gives it a great advantage over the countries of Europe, whose nationhood is founded at least to some extent on a socio-biological past and which therefore have much greater difficulty, both conceptually and in practice, in absorbing and acculturating large numbers of immigrants. America is thus free of the nastier forms of nationalism that have pullulated in Europe in the past, and could easily pullulate there again.[84]

Third, there is American religious belief. Perhaps because no church has ever been established in the United States, religion has survived there better than in countries where religious belief has been closely associated with the temporal power. Once the power to enforce conformity and suppress dissent declines in countries where there has been a state religion, religious belief itself declines precipitately, for it is seen as having sided with the wrong side of history. For constitutional reasons, there is no danger of this in the United States; and the religiosity of the Americans keeps alive the little platoons that are so important in maintaining the health and vigor of civil society independent of the government.

---

84. France is a partial, but only a partial, exception to the non-ideological (or non-philosophical) nature of European nation states. As its current president pointed out, its republicanism phase is only a part, and a small part at that, of its immemorial existence. The republican phase, moreover, coincided with the development of France's overseas empire, an empire that could hardly have been more in contradiction with its philosophical republicanism. Of course, slavery was also in contradiction to the founding principles of American republicanism; but the Americans rid themselves of this contradiction by their civil war (whether or not the war was fought over emancipation), whereas the French Republic lost its overseas empire against its own will. The French might indeed have taught African children to say "Nos ancêtres, les gaulois," but colonial practice gave the lie to this historical metaphor.

Finally, there is American military power, which is unprecedented both in the nation's and the world's history. America spends more on its military than the rest of the world combined. This should secure its predominance for the foreseeable future.

In short, the United States is free, or nearly so, from the principal factors that have led to the decline and immobilism of Europe, its sclerosis, rigidity, and lack of ability to confront the challenges facing it. And, since nothing is inevitable, this may yet prove to be the case.

It is not, however, certain. Like Europeans, Americans have not proved deeply attached to limited government, and the difference between Europe and America in this respect is only one of degree rather than of type. The notion that individual Americans are jealous of their economic independence and intellectual liberty to an extent quite different from that of the people of other nations is no more true than that the Australians, who live in the most urbanized society in the world, are a nation of Crocodile Dundees. Irrespective of whether the extension of government power in the current economic crisis is economically wise or not, it is not meeting much resistance from the population or its representatives. It is hardly too much to say that, at least temporarily, the leaders of American life have placed an almost religious faith in a man who, in so far as he is not wholly untested, promises to extend the role of the American state in everybody's life.

The religiosity of the Americans strikes foreigners as superficial and as much a kind of communal psychotherapy as a genuine faith. (Of course, any generalization about 300,000,000 people must have its exceptions, who in aggregate are numerous). American religion is Dale Carnegie transposed to a mildly, and unconvincingly, transcendental plane; a lot of American religious services are like meetings of Alcoholics Anonymous without the alcoholics.

Military power is often if not illusory, at least of limited use, especially when nations have scruples. Where a public opinion exists, as it undoubtedly still does in the United States, the full force of military power is under a restraint and cannot be employed on the task of limitless repression. Moreover, there are in any case inherent limits to what raw physical power can achieve. The most powerful man in the world cannot mold the weakest entirely to his will, and this is because of the most glorious of human qualities: human freedom. I do not mean here the freedom that arises from constitutional arrangements, but a much deeper, existential freedom: the freedom to choose how you react to circumstances. A tyrant can change the circumstances, but not fully determine the reaction to them. As European colonialists in Africa discovered, the powerful can change the weak, but not according to their will or design (and for this we may thank God, for otherwise the nightmare of total control of populations might be implementable).

History suggests that world predominance, however solid it may appear, does not last forever. It is at least possible that China will become a military power if not superior to the United States, at least sufficiently great to limit its freedom. Even now, I think it highly doubtful that, if China chose to invade Taiwan, the United States would intervene militarily. Against China's relatively small military budget must be set the huge wage bill of the American military. The relationship between military expenditure, military power, and the ability to impose military solutions is not direct.

Recent events have shown that the United States is not immune from economic laws. By means of the extension of cheap credit resulting in asset inflation, its government has sought to create the illusion of private prosperity while increasing public expenditure. As the emitter of the world's reserve currency, it behaved as if it believed foreign debt could be accumulated forever without in the end losing control of the fate of that currency. For a long time during the Cold War, the military doctrine was one of Mutual Assured Destruction (MAD); now the United States finds itself in the same position *vis-à-vis* China with regard to the dollar. For the moment, the interests of both countries coincide, but there is no guarantee that this equilibrium of interests will last indefinitely.

In many respects, then, the United States is not in so different a position from that of Europe. The demographics of its core population are not very different from those of Europe: the natality of the population of European descent is below replacement level. It has a welfare state that can easily be expanded to European levels, and (at the present time) it looks as if this is likely to happen. Once established, that state is difficult to dismantle because of the vested interests that have been created.[85] The United States, therefore, like Europe, might soon find itself oscillating endlessly between the necessity and impossibility of reducing the scope and reach of the welfare state. If the welfare state reaches European levels in the United States, one of its decisive advantages over Europe–its ability to assimilate immigrants—will disappear.

The United States finds itself at a historical conjuncture when its relative power in the world has weakened. To be sure, no decline in power comparable in extent to that of Europe in the twentieth century is in view; nevertheless, the realization of this weakening, that the United States is re-entering a world in which it is only *primum inter pares* and not utterly dominant, might cause disappointment to those who see the cup of power dashed from their lips. Self-hatred and self-denigration might then take hold with disastrous wider effect.

As we have seen, the European loss of power coincided with the spread of an ideologically miserabilist interpretation of its own history.[86] This was for obvious historical reasons: nevertheless, it is important to remember that no such reading of history is compelled by the evidence, that it is chosen for other reasons. As we

---

85. The Swedish Social Democrats understood this well. They understood that once the total number of people dependent upon the welfare state, either directly as recipients of assistance or indirectly as employees of the apparatus that distributed it, reached 51 percent, change would be exceedingly difficult to bring about, even for an opposition. This was borne out when the conservative opposition in Sweden campaigned on an anti-welfare state program. It was annihilated at the polls. When it promised to change very little, it was elected. In Britain, Mrs. Thatcher made scarcely any inroads into the welfare state. It was as much as she could do to reduce the power and influence of the trade unions, and even this much lesser task caused enormous social conflict. From lack of political capital after the struggle with the unions, she left the welfare state intact. By introducing managerialism into the state apparatus, she corrupted it to a degree unseen since the eighteenth century. Of this process, Anthony Blair, her ultimate successor, was able to take full advantage. A man of consummate dishonesty, legalized corruption was not only a consequence of his policy: it was the whole of his policy.

86. Historical miserabilism may be defined as the view that all has always been for the worst in this, the worst of all possible worlds. On this view, achievements count for nothing and are taken for granted, while disasters are magnified and kept constantly at the forefront of the mind.

have seen, intellectuals, not primarily historians, had a decisive influence on the way in which the First World War was subsequently interpreted, an influence that extends to our day.

A combination of loss of power and historiographical miserabilism leaves a society in poor condition to maintain its social fabric. On the face of it, the history of the United States is less susceptible to a miserabilist interpretation than that of most countries. But miserabilism is never compelled by the evidence alone, and intellectual ingenuity can always descry the cloud in any silver lining. America could be described as a state founded first on genocide and then on slave-owning hypocrisy, that subsequently appropriated half of Mexico, etc., etc. Grievance-mongers can project their current discontents backwards and easily demonstrate that America has been a paradise for racists, sexists, persecutors of homosexuals, etc. Corruption has always been rife in it, jobbing politicians have always led the population by the nose. Even the disillusionment that will inevitably follow the euphoria of Mr. Obama's election will be grist to the miserabilist mill.

This is not, of course, to call for an equal and opposite historiography, in which there is nothing but a glorious upward ascent and everything American is best. One of the dangers of this kind of historiography is that, when disillusionment comes, it is total. And such a disillusionment is particularly strong when the pride in power, with which it is often associated, receives the unpleasant shock that the power has evaporated.

Rather, a defense of all that is best, and of all the achievement, in American history is necessary. That is why the outcome of the so-called culture wars in America is so important to its future. A healthy modern society must know how to remain the same as well as change, to conserve as well as to reform. Europe has changed without knowing how to conserve: that is its tragedy.

INDEX